D0119424

An Illustrated History of
BRITISH RAILWAYS'
WORKSHOPS

'Claughton' 4-6-0 No. 1327 *Sir Frederick Harrison* being transported by two 40-ton cranes in late LNWR days at Crewe Works. On the right is 'George the Fifth' class 4-4-0 No. 1644 *Roebuck*. The name *Sir Frederick Harrison* was later carried by two "Baby Scot" 'Patriot' class 4-6-0s, LMS Nos 5524 and 5531 successively. No. 5531 was one of the first "Baby Scots" to be rebuilt by the LMS with a large 2A taper boiler and double chimney, etc.

(National Railway Museum)

Also by Edgar J. Larkin

Works Organisation and Management
The Elements of Workshop Training
Memoirs of a Railway Engineer
The Railway Workshops of Britain, 1823-1986

The larger locomotive works had the machines and skills to manufacture a vast range of products, including machinery, such as this massive hydraulic press which was made in the works at Crewe in 1899. It is seen here shaping a steel fillet in 1901. The versatility of the railway shops was well exploited during both world wars to carry out very specialised war work.

(National Railway Musuem)

Title page: Inside Brighton Works on 2nd October 1954, BR Standard Class 4MT 2-6-4T No. 80094 is under construction whilst, alongside, ex-LMS diesel-electric No. 10000 receives attention, just a few months prior to being transferred back to the London Midland Region. Brighton were responsible for building 130 of the 155 Class 4 tanks (the balance emanating from Derby) and this view is interesting as the front plating has not yet been fixed and the integral construction of the smokebox saddle and exhaust steam-pipe is revealed.

(Brian Morrison)

An Illustrated History of
BRITISH RAILWAYS' WORKSHOPS

Locomotive, Carriage and Wagon Building and Maintenance, from 1825 to the Present Day

EDGAR LARKIN

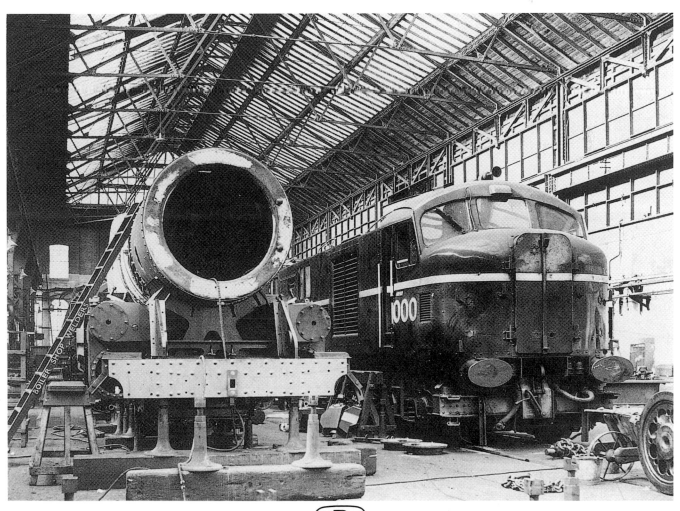

OPC

Oxford Publishing Co.

Apprentice riveter riviting a smokebox to the saddle flange in the Boiler Shop at Bow Works.

First edition
© 1992 E. J. Larkin & Haynes Publishing Group
Reprinted 2006
All rights reserved. No part of this book may be reproduced or
transmitted in any form or by any means, electronic or mechanical,
including photocopying, recording or by any information storage or
retrieval system, without written permission from the copyright
owner.

A catalogue record for this book is available from the British Library

ISBN 0-86093-503-5

Library of Congress catalog card number
92–72548

Oxford Publishing Co. is part of the
Haynes Publishing Group
Sparkford, Near Yeovil, Somerset, BA22 7JJ

Haynes Publications Inc.
861 Lawrence Drive, Newbury Park, California 91320, USA

Printed in China
Reprinted 2007

Contents

Foreword

by

F.G. Clements MBE, C.ENG., F.I.MECH. E.
Formerly Chief Mechanical and Electrical Engineer,
of the Scottish Region, and subsequently
of the London Midland Region of British Railways

During my early career as an Engineering Apprentice in the LMS Horwich Works, I came to the notice of Edgar Larkin, at the Derby Headquarters of my Department, when he approved of my transfer from the Works to the Motive Power Department.

I was always impressed with Edgar's progress through the Railway Industry. Over a period of years he was Chairman of no less than seven British Railways Policy Committees directly associated with the monumental fifteen years £1,600 million Reorganisation Plan of British Railways, as approved by the Government in 1954. Included in this was the reorganisation of the Works management at each of the Main Works, and Edgar first chaired the Locomotive Works Committee, followed by a corresponding committee of the Carriage and Wagon Works.

Another committee which Edgar chaired was the Spare Parts Committee for Diesel and Electric Traction, involving an expenditure of several million pounds.

In 1955 Edgar was seconded to the British Transport Commission to report directly to the Chairman, Lord Robertson, on the urgent need for additional well qual-ified mechanical and electrical engineers, and also to provide a vital Instructional Centre to meet the requirements of the fifteen years British Railways Modernisation Plan.

During his time as Deputy General Manager of the newly-formed British Railways Workshops Division in 1962, which employed a total staff of 60,000, Edgar introduced a modern production planning system for the manufacture of locomotives, carriages and wagons at each of the Works involved in new manufacture.

He is a Fellow of the Institution of Mechanical Engineers and was awarded the OBE in 1961.

As a side interest Edgar Larkin has been a quite prolific writer of technical literature over the many years of his life, the earliest of which in 1941, entitled *Works Organisation and Management*, and which ran to a second edition, was of considerable help to me in Industry and in my studies.

It is fitting that he should be "signing off" at the age of ninety-two years, with such a unique photographic and historical record of the Railway Workshops of Britain.

F. G. Clements

Abbreviations of Railway Companies

BR	British Railways/British Rail		
BREL	British Rail Engineering Limited	LNWR	London & North Western Railway
BTC	British Transport Commission	LSWR	London & South Western Railway
CR	Caledonian Railway	LYR	Lancashire & Yorkshire Railway
ECR	Eastern Counties Railway	MR	Midland Railway
G&SWR	Glasgow & South Western Railway	MSLR	Manchester, Sheffield & Lincolnshire Railway
GCR	Great Central Railway	NBR	North British Railway
GER	Great Eastern Railway	NER	North Eastern Railway
GJR	Grand Junction Railway	NLR	North London Railway
GNR	Great Northern Railway	NMR	North Midland Railway
GNSR	Great North of Scotland Railway	S&BR	Shrewsbury & Birmingham Railway
GWR	Great Western Railway	S&DR	Stockton & Darlington Railway
LBSCR	London, Brighton & South Coast Railway	SECR	South Eastern & Chatham Railway
LMSR	London, Midland & Scottish Railway	SER	South Eastern Railway
LNER	London & North Eastern Railway	SR	Southern Railway

Acknowledgements

In the early stages of this book the author's only son, John Garth Larkin MA, LL.M., put together a wealth of basic information, as well as assembling most of the photographs suitable for this publication. Subsequently colleagues on British Railways made substantial contributions. They are James M. Jarvis, M.Sc., C. Eng., M.I.Mech.E., a Locomotive Engineer, who provided the introductory story and photograph captions for the Locomotive Section, and H. R. Roberts, S.B.St.J., C.Eng., F.I.Mech.E., formerly Works Manager at Swindon, who contributed the write-up and photograph captions for Carriages and Freight Vehicles.

Well-known railway colleagues and other friends also contributed and enhanced the value of this unique railway book, and the author expresses his sincere thanks to the undermentioned for their respective contributions. Gerald J. Aston MA, FCIT, C.P. Atkins, Librarian at the National Railway Museum, York, John Barker-Wyatt E.R.D., T.D., C.Eng., F.I.Mech.E., Winifred Collins, Alec H. Emerson C.Eng., F.I.Mech.E., F.I.E.E., John D. Forster, J.A. Higton, J.R. Hillier, Geoff Holme and Cumbrian Railways Association, Peter Holmes, Janet Kierton, Roger Larkam B.Sc., my nephew Peter J. Larkin, R.C.S. Low M.C., M.B.E., B.Sc., C.Eng., F.I.Mech.E., Dennis J. Lees B.Sc., G.H.D. Mackie O.B.E., O.St.J., C.Eng., F.I.Mech.E., F.C.I.T., Colin J. Marsden, Brian Morrison, S.G. Morrison, Librarian at the Institution of Mechanical Engineers, Peter Nicholson, Editor of OPC, F. Ogden, P.S.M. Ramsey, Lance Sanders, Robin Stables M.A. (CANTAB), C. Eng., F.I.Mech. E. and I am indebted to Karen Jenkins for all the clerical and typing work involved.

Fig 1. Map showing the location of BR's Main Works.

Preface

A book of this character, covering a period of no less than 167 years, is very special. It is unique as a pictorial record of the railway workshops within the British Isles, from the days of Trevithick and the Stephensons, to the advanced workshops of British Rail.

Over the years many informative books have been published about British Railways, but until the publication of the author's *The Railway Workshops of Britain, 1823–1986* (Macmillan 1988), none had depicted the development of the main works and their products from the earliest days to the present time. This comprehensive volume now provides the reader with a broadly based photographic record of the railway's workshops and their products, looking primarily at those surviving into BR days. It is an authoritative, historical and fascinating story which will appeal to mechanical and electrical engineers and railway enthusiasts alike.

Within British Railways a Main Works has always been classified as one which is equipped to build, and, or undertake, heavy classified repairs of locomotives, carriages, or freight vehicles.

There are many local Motive Power Depots, Carriage Repair Depots and Freight Repair Depots where light classified repairs are undertaken and which do not involve haulage to a Main Works, nor require high cost workshops equipment.

In recent years the Main Works have been closed and the workload transferred to British Rail depots and to private contractors. This has been the result of implementing the British Rail Manufacturing and Maintenance Policy for locomotives, carriages, and wagons, as published in May 1986.

In some of the railway towns all three activities, locomotives, carriages and freight vehicles were undertaken. In total there were 49 Main Works centres as follows:

Locomotives	18
Carriages	14
Wagons	17
Total	49

In reviewing the relationship between private contractors manufacturing new traction and rolling stock, British Rail's own main works in BREL, and the maintenance depots, it was concluded that whilst British Rail needed to retain control over its maintenance depots because their work was intimately connected with running the railway, the activities of heavy repair and new manufacture could be provided for British Rail on a contract basis. However British Rail would need to involve itself directly in the purchasing and warehousing of material to support depot maintenance activities. Thus during 1986–87 the transfer of light and intermediate repair from BREL to British Rail depots took place but BR retained Glasgow, Doncaster and Wolverton (all on a very much reduced scale) and Eastleigh Works. A BR National Store for material was established at Doncaster.

To support light and intermediate overhaul of vehicles in depots, a policy of component exchange was introduced, with British Rail contracting the overhaul of components eg diesel engines, to BREL or private contractors. The BREL activity in Crewe, Derby and York became more and more at arms length to British Rail, and in April 1989 was sold to a consortium of major companies and senior members of BREL. The large mechanised foundry at Horwich was sold separately in 1988.

Today all that exists of the British Railways Main Works in BR ownership is Eastleigh and parts of the Main Works in Glasgow, Doncaster and Wolverton under the title British Rail Maintenance Limited. The latter works has the distinction of continuing the building and maintenance of the Royal Train.

The Horwich Works erecting shop in 1957 was assembling British Railways Standard Class 4 2-6-0s. 115 of these mixed traffic engines were built from 1952–57, to a design based on Ivatt's LMS class, numbering 162, of which nearly half had also been built at Horwich.

1

The Beginning of Railways

The history of the railways of Britain is a unique and fascinating story. It began in 1825 with the opening of the Stockton & Darlington Railway, a distance of twenty miles, when George Stephenson's locomotive named *Locomotion* hauled the first steam driven train in the world on a public railway, carrying a load of eighty tons of coal from the mines at Stockton to the town of Darlington.

In 1829, four years later, the Liverpool & Manchester Railway, 33 miles long, was completed and was the first steam worked passenger carrying railway. In 1830 the proprietors of the day organised the world famous Rainhill Trials with a view to ascertaining the most suitable type of motive power for the projected railway. There were five competitors, as follows:

The *Rocket*, entered by George and Robert Stephenson and Henry Booth.
The *Novelty*, by John Braithwaite and John Ericsson.

The *Sans Pareil* by Timothy Hackworth.
The *Perseverance* by Timothy Burstall
The *Cyclopede* by T.S. Brandreth, which was worked by a pair of horses.

On 8th October 1829 *Rocket* carried out the required test and put up a near faultless performance. It completed the distance at an average speed of 16 mph, with a maximum of 29 mph. Thus was settled the question of the power to be employed on railways; for a century at all events. The *Rocket* cost £550, weighed 4½ tons and was required to draw 9½ tons behind the tender for seventy miles at ten miles per hour.

The winner of the contest *Rocket*, had the distinction of hauling the first passenger train on 13th September 1830 at the official opening of the line by the Prime Minister, the Duke of Wellington.

A scene from the Pageant of Transport, organised by the LMS in 1930 to mark the centenary of the opening of the Liverpool & Manchester Railway.

Derby Locomotive Works in September 1991 from the roof of Railway Technical Centre building, with RTC sidings in the foreground.

(Colin J. Marsden)

A hundred years later *Royal Scot* cost £8,000, weighed 85 tons without the tender and pulled 400 tons for 400 miles at an average speed of nearly a mile a minute. The railways have made astonishing progress since those pioneering days.

Following the opening of the Stockton & Darlington Railway and the Liverpool & Manchester Railway, other railways were started in Britain, and by 1923 there was a total of 120 independent railway companies, some of them already an amalgamation of two or more railway companies. As from 1st January 1923 the Government passed an historic Act which amalgamated these 120 companies into four companies, namely the Great Western Railway, the London, Midland & Scottish Railway, the London & North Eastern Railway, and the Southern Railway. Twenty-five years later, on 1st January 1948, these four companies were nationalised and organised into six Regions. Subsequently, the Eastern and North Eastern Regions were amalgamated to form the Eastern Region. Thus BR was an amalgamation of five Regions, and in descending order of size, where the LMR, ER, WR, SR and the ScR.

At first the Liverpool & Manchester Railway had no facilities for building the new forms of motive power and bought them from a growing number of firms in England. As time went on, most of the newly formed railway companies built their own locomotives and rolling stock and the established manufacturers concentrated more on building for overseas.

It is fascinating to put on record that in 1923, the year of the amalgamation, the 'Big Four' had the highest total of locomotives and rolling stock in the history of Britain's railways.

The indispensable Record Office of British Railways is located in Derby. All alterations in design and mileage covered are accurately recorded and kept up-to-date. The peak year for the maximum number of stock and receipts was 1948 (the year of Nationalisation).

In 1988, some forty years later, the stock, due to the dramatic and almost unbelievable influx of road and air traffic in such a relatively short time, had fallen, as shown in Appendix VII to as little as 6% of the previous maximum. This striking contrast has not been published before as far as I know.

2

Locomotives and Power Units

Steam locomotives have had an entirely beneficial effect for mankind, and played a leading part in the spread of trade, populations and civilisation in various countries, particularly the Americas in the 19th Century.

Britain was responsible for developing the first railway locomotives in the early 1800s, and the products of engineers such as Trevithick, Blenkinsop and Hedley operated on industrial tramways with varying success. These pioneers were followed by Timothy Hackworth and George Stephenson and his son Robert. It is generally acknowledged that the *Rocket* was the first steam locomotive to combine the essential features which subsequently comprised orthodox practice until the final days of steam. In particular the exhaust steam from the cylinders was used to create the draught through a large number of fire tubes in the boiler. In this way the intensity of fire in the firebox was raised as the power output of the cylinders increased, thereby helping to match the supply of steam to its demand.

The success of the Liverpool & Manchester Railway led to the very rapid growth of railways for carrying passengers and freight hauled by steam traction not only in Britain, but in Europe and North America, and subsequently elsewhere.

Over the years steam engines became larger, more powerful and efficient and incorporated additional sophisticated features. Ramsbottom of the London & North Western Railway introduced piston rings in 1858 which greatly reduced steam leakage past the pistons and he was the first to introduce injectors in Britain, which became a favoured alternative to feed pumps of various types.

Whilst the number of wheels under the locomotive increased, it was not until the 20th Century that 4-4-2, 2-6-0, 4-6-0, 0-8-0 and 2-8-0 wheel arrangements began to appear in any significant numbers in Britain, and not until the 1920s that 4-6-2s and 2-8-2s were introduced, initially under Gresley of the GNR and then LNER (apart from the GWR's short-lived *Great Bear* of 1908 and a few tank engines.

Boiler Design. Boiler size increased steadily as did the working pressure in order to meet the ever-rising demand for more power. Narrow fireboxes reaching down between the plate frames were the norm, until the new 4-4-2 express engines on the Great Northern and London, Brighton & South Coast Railways arrived in the early 1900s with wide fireboxes, to be followed by Gresley's 4-6-2s and 2-8-2s and various more-recent Pacifics and BR Class 9 2-10-0s.

In the early years of the 20th Century great technical advances in design and maintenance were made by Churchward of the GWR, who incorporated good practices from America and France for his range of standard types, using many common components. He introduced long-travel, long-lap piston valves, smoother and more direct steam passages, American-style cylinder design and smokebox saddles, together with greatly improved boiler proportions and performance. Unfortunately, it was a considerable time before the other British railways took heed of these advances. In most cases only some time after the Grouping of 1923.

Whilst Churchward made the first British-use of Schmidt fire-tube superheaters in 1905, the Great Western Railway for many years used only very moderate superheat. The Lancashire & Yorkshire Railway was the first to fit high degree superheaters in 1906. This feature was quickly adopted by most railways on their new larger engines and fitted to many existing classes, often reducing steam and coal consumptions by around 20%. Superheating in its turn virtually required the use of piston valves to avoid the problem of adequately lubricating slide valves at the higher working temperatures.

During the 19th Century and the first part of the 20th, a high proportion of British locomotives had inside cylinders, fitted between the frames and below the smokebox, their motion driving onto a crank axle. More recently, most new designs, except for tank engines used for shunting or short trip working, incorporated outside cylinders, although a number of more powerful types needing three or four cylinders had inside cylinders as well. Outside cylinders provided better accessibility to the motion, and mitigated the problem on powerful locomotives of providing large enough axlebox bearings in a crank axle, which by its geometry caused larger and more horizontal peak thrusts on the bearings.

Walschaerts Valve Gear. Walschaerts valve gear, which was particularly suited to outside cylinders, became increasingly used after the First World War, in place of the previously predominant Stephenson gear, amongst other rarer types. On the LNER, Gresley introduced a simple arrangement of levers for operating the inside cylinder's valves from the two sets of outside valve gears. Several varieties of poppet valves were fitted to a limited series of engines on the LNER, LMS and finally, BR.

During and subsequent to the Second World War, there was a firm need to reduce maintenance and servicing requirements to a minimum, which encouraged the use of outside cylinders only, as far as possible, on new designs. It also prompted the introduction of new features such as roller bearing axleboxes, rocking grates, hopper ash pans and self-cleaning smokeboxes, as well as wear resistant materials, such as manganese steel, to reduce wear on the faces of axleboxes and hornblocks which had to slide against each other. Over the years, great improvements and simplifications were made in the design of bearings for axleboxes and the main motion components, such as connecting and coupling rods. This was made possible by more modern machining techniques, and lubrication arrangements were also steadily improved. As a result the incidence of hot axleboxes in modern locomotives was drastically reduced to an almost negligible level.

Loading Gauge. In being first with introducing railways, Britain was saddled with a more restrictive loading gauge resulting from the limited size of early bridges and tunnels and its adoption of high station platforms. In consequence Britain's own locomotives never reached the size and power achieved in many other countries whose railways were developed later. This restriction may well have been a factor in discouraging the use of compounding on new designs of large locomotives because of the greater difficulty in accommodating large low pressure cylinders. Unlike various other countries, particularly France, Britain had only one long lasting large class of compound engines, namely the Midland/LMS 4-4-0s built at Derby and by contractors between 1902 and 1932, and which all lasted into the 1950s and early '60s. Previously the London & North Western Railway, under Webb's regime, had operated a range of ineffective compound classes for a limited period, only to be superseded or rebuilt to simple expansion. Some other railways also tried compounding on a few engines. Except for some isolated trials, mechanical stokers were never adopted on Britain's locomotives because their limited size and output did not distinctly justify the feature, with its cost and complication.

Articulated locomotives did not find much favour in Britain, the only main-line examples being the LNER Garratt banker built by Beyer, Peacock in 1925, and the 33 LMS heavy freight Garratts made by the same firm from 1927-1930.

Railway Manufacture. The railways in Britain, more so than in other countries, designed and built in their own workshops a high proportion of their locomotives, in addition to carrying out regular repair work. As a result there was a wide range of classes, and distinctive differences in design and appearance between the various railways, not to mention significant changes that often occurred after a fresh locomotive chief took charge. Likewise the performance and efficiency of different locomotive fleets varied greatly.

British steam engines were renowned for their generally clean, uncluttered appearance, and from the mid 19th Century much care had been given to providing most of them with shapely outlines and features, enhanced, especially prior to the First World War, by various colourful liveries and decorative lining-out. Later, the need for economy and more intensive working inevitably caused a decline in embellishment and cleanliness. More recently, the trend to greater functional design to improve accessibility of fittings and pipework, etc., undoubtedly detracted from the earlier gracefulness, but beauty lies in the eye of the beholder, and a business-like steam engine can still look very attractive.

This is not the place to review the various attempts in Britain and elsewhere to evolve types of steam locomotives more efficient and economic than the conventional ones. Suffice it to say that virtually none of them made the grade sufficiently to convince any Railway to persevere with them. The Stephenson concept held sway because of its low first cost, simplicity, robustness and effectiveness until it was overtaken by non-steam traction.

In conclusion the conventional steam locomotive was a robust machine comprising several closely inter-

Progress Office, Derby Locomotive Works in the 1930s.

Derby Works first diesel locomotive, No. 1831 being wheeled in February 1934.
(Colin J. Marsden Collection)

related major components, such as the boiler, the cylinders and engine motion, and the smokebox front end and steam passages. Their relationship needed to be well balanced to achieve optimum performance and efficiency which were also significantly dependent on the skill and effective teamwork of the footplate crew, and the quality of the fuel, particularly where this was coal. In consequence, the power output in actual service was neither closely predictable nor consistent, and fresh designs of locomotive needed trials or more scientific testing to establish their potential, and in a number of cases some modifications to draughting arrangements to improve 'steaming'. On the other hand, unless some really major fault occurred, a steam locomotive could usually complete its journey albeit by limping home!

In contrast, the main items of power equipment in diesel and electric locomotives, which are to be considered next, normally perform predictably in producing and transmitting their output. The result is that the power performance of the locomotive can be accurately forecast at the design stage, and achieved consistently in service, providing the locomotive remains in satisfactory condition. Therefore, these locomotives are much less susceptible to the temperaments both of their own machinery and the crew. However, such motive power can become completely immobilised by the malfunction of some obscure component, such as an electrical relay, and at times the fault can take longer to trace than to rectify.

The story of non-steam locomotives is still unfolding, but the railways and their workshops have led a less dominant role in their evolution, as the important traction machinery, such as diesel engines and electrical and transmission equipment, has been wisely left in the hands of the specialised manufacturers, who in a high proportion of cases also designed and constructed the locomotives as well.

Diesel Locomotives. In Britain the LMS Railway led the way in pioneering diesel shunting locomotives, operating a variety of specimens as the 1930s progressed, finally settling on the 350hp diesel-electric 0-6-0 as the standard. Broadly similar locomotives

were also acquired by the other main-line railway companies, and BR developed the same design for its large orders; manufacture of mechanical parts and assembly being carried out in its own workshops. BR also ordered various makes of lower powered shunters, mainly having mechanical transmission, plus over 200 built in its works.

The LMS under H.G. Ivatt again pioneered in the case of main-line diesel locomotives, building in its own Derby Works during 1947/8 two 1,600 hp diesel-electric locomotives Nos 10000 and 10001, using English Electric diesel engines and electrical equipment. It is an illustration of the extensive resources and determination of that railway that it was able to design (apart from earlier scheming) and construct in less than a year, the first of those two machines, which were entirely novel in relation to the railway's experience in respect of both the drawing office and the workshops. Nevertheless, the locomotives were substantially very successful. The Southern Railway followed closely by authorising two 1,750 hp locomotives using similar power equipments in a somewhat different chassis and bogie concept, construction being undertaken in Brighton Works in BR days. A third locomotive rated at 2,000 hp followed a few years later.

Derby also designed and built an unusual diesel-mechanical locomotive incorporating a multi-engine and gearbox arrangement evolved by Col. Fell and about the same time a more conventional 800 hp Bo-Bo diesel electric locomotive was ordered from the North British Locomotive Co.

Useful experience was gained with operating these machines, but initially, the economic case for widespread main-line diesel traction did not seem too promising, bearing in mind the much higher capital costs of such units and the then much lower cost of coal which virtually offset the higher efficiency of diesels. Furthermore, the Railway Executive did not feel it wise to rely heavily on imported oil fuel, and considered steam should be steadily replaced by electrification.

Whilst the use of diesel shunting locomotives was being extended, and diesel multiple unit trains were being introduced to take over local and branch line services, it was not until the unparalleled Railway Modernisation Plan of 1954/5, involving an expenditure of £1,600 million, was announced under the new management which replaced the Railway Executive, that a bold step forward was made towards main-line diesel and electric operation. A total of 174 locomotives of several power groups was ordered, involving most of the principal British locomotive manufacturers, and incorporating various types of diesel engine, and electrical and hydraulic transmissions. The purpose was to carry out a widespread trial for several years in order to establish the best designs and features to incorporate in future bulk orders. In the event, such engineering considerations were forestalled by the British Transport Commission insisting on an earlier and faster introduction of diesels, involving further orders being placed before any real experience in service had been obtained with the pilot orders. On top of the technical disadvantages caused, the sheer scale and speed of the changeover created severe difficulties in training staff and providing proper facilities to take care of the new type of traction.

Whilst most of the initial and later classes were designed by the manufacturers, Derby design office dealt with two sizes of diesel-electric locomotives, which were built in several railway workshops. Swindon undertook the preparation of two sophisticated designs of diesel-hydraulic locomotive based on German practice, and subsequently for a smaller 650 hp locomotive for local trip and yard working.

By this time, the design of diesel-electric locomotive chassis and superstructure had become more formalised and familiar, and was no longer the adventure it had been in the cases of the original LMS and SR prototypes. Nevertheless, there were plenty of interesting problems to overcome, not least keeping the overall weight in check and meeting the Chief Civil Engineer's stringent requirements for the ratio of wheel loading to wheel diameter.

Doncaster, Brighton and Ashford drawing offices designed some dc electric locomotives prior to Nationalisation and subsequently further classes under the Modernisation Plan. Doncaster was then allocated some of the new 25kV ac classes. Brighton also designed the ingenious electro-diesel locomotives, which have proved so versatile and useful over the Southern Region's system.

In the latter 1960s BR's own major design work was concentrated at the Railway Technical Centre, Derby, until during the 1980s when the Railway discontinued this activity, passing the responsibility to the manufacturers, so that British Rail Engineering took over most of the design staff to carry out design work for its own tendering, to meet the detailed specifications of BR.

One of the most notable achievements of the era has been the development of the InterCity 125 High Speed Trains, whose diesel power cars, although officially regarded as part of the integral trains, are, in effect, single-ended locomotives. Their design had to be very carefully prepared in order to meet the severe restrictions on axleloads imposed as a condition for running at 125 mph. These trains, progressively introduced on various non-electrified key routes, soon transformed the speed and standard of service wherever they operated, and played a major part in revitalising BR's passenger business.

Other main design projects have been the updating of the Class 87 ac electric locomotive design for further construction as Class 90; the development of the Class 58 heavy freight diesel locomotives, and designing the production versions of the ill-fated Advanced Passenger Train.

During the 1980s the Railway divested itself of new design activity and concentrated on preparing detailed business specifications to which manufacturers, including British Rail Engineering Limited, produced their own designs and tendered for traction and rolling stock construction.

With the recent privatisation of the remaining major railway workshops, the long and fascinating story of locomotive, carriage and wagon construction in the railway-owned works has come to an end.

A sequence of views showing the construction of Stanier 3-cylinder 2-6-4T No. 2528 in Derby Locomotive Works in 1934.

Locomotive Works
Acquired by British Railways, 1948

| Location | Date Built | Owning Company | | Date of Closure |
		Pre 1923	Post 1923	
Ashford	1847	SECR	SR	1962
Bow	1850	NLR	LMSR	1960
Brighton	1840	LBSCR	SR	1964
Caerphilly	1899	RR	GWR	1963
Cowlairs	1842	NBR	LNER	1968
Crewe	1843	LNWR	LMSR	–
Darlington	1863	NER	LNER	1966
Derby	1840	MR	LMSR	–
Doncaster	1853	GNR	LNER	–
Eastleigh	1909	LSWR	SR	–
Gorton	1849	MSLR/GCR	LNER	1962
Horwich	1887	LYR	LMSR	1968
Inverurie	1903	GNSR	LNER	1969
Kilmarnock	1856	GSWR	LMSR	1959
St Rollox	1856	CR	LMSR	–
Stratford	1847	ECR/GER	LNER	1962
Swindon	1842	GWR	GWR	1986
Wolverhampton	1855	GWR	GWR	1964

Pre-Grouping Locomotive Works

In addition to the Works that were handed over to the BTC at Nationalisation on 1st January 1948, there were many locomotive workshops that had been closed previously or reduced considerably in their importance. Some of those of the earlier railway companies had been superseded by later, more modern works or had been the subject of rationalisation by the pre-Nationalisation companies.

Although detailed descriptions of these Works are outside the scope of the first edition of this book, a brief mention needs to be made of some, as their names live on and will be known to many today. This is because locomotives built by the following works have survived into the present day through preservation:

Gateshead Works, Co. Durham. Newcastle & Darlington Junction Railway/York, Newcastle & Berwick Railway/North Eastern Railway/LNER 1844 – 1932 (Re-opened for repair work only, 1939 – 1959.)

Longhedge Works, London. London, Chatham & Dover Railway/South Eastern & Chatham Railway 1862 – 1911.

Nine Elms Works, London. London & South Western Railway 1839 – 1909.

Stoke Works, Stoke-on-Trent, Staffordshire. North Staffordshire Railway/LMSR 1868 – 1927.

West Yard Works, Cardiff. Taff Vale Railway/GWR 1840s – 1926.

Edited Extracts from the Locomotive Works Organisation Report, December 1948.

Summary of Practices for the Control of New Manufacturing Activities.

It has been the practice on all the four Main Line Companies for the authorisation of new engine building programmes or 'New Work' schemes of a major character to rest primarily with each Chief Mechanical Engineer and, so far as the Workshops are concerned, the authority given by him forms the basis for the Works procedure. In all cases the initiation of such work is controlled by the issue of local Works orders by the Works Managers, fully describing the work to be put in hand, and providing the origin for subsequent work-controlling documents.

The authority for the manufacture of stock replenishments is given by the Stores Superintendent or his local representative.

The procedure for control subsequent to the issue of either a Works order or stock order, however, varies considerably and there are many differences in the extent to which process planning, issue of work-authorising documents, fixing of piecework prices and progress of work are co-ordinated functions. On the former LMS Rly there exists at all the larger Main Works a Production Planning Organisation which co-ordinates all the functions mentioned, but in the Works of the other railways, the functions are delegated to the Shop supervisory staff or to separate sections of the Works Manager's organisation.

The control of expenditure as it is incurred is, of course, largely within the scope of the functions mentioned above but, in addition, the ex-GW, LMS and Southern Rlys have systems of control which, by continuous scrutiny of both wages and material charges, check that work is being performed within the authorised expenditure. The ex-LNE Rly have, of recent origin, a system of budgetary control which gives close supervision of expenditure, particularly expenditure of an indirect nature. This is being extended to embrace a system of direct cost control by the derivation and use of standard costs for all items produced.

CONTROL OF THE PROGRESS OF LOCOMOTIVE REPAIRS.

Ex-Great Western Railway

The following describes the method in use at Swindon, but the principle applies also at Wolverhampton and Caerphilly, with modifications to suit the much smaller size of these Works.

On arrival at the Works, locomotives are placed in the 'Factory Pool', whence they are drawn as instructed by the Assistant to Works Manager (Locomotive Maintenance and New Work) to the Engine Reception Shop. Here they receive a preliminary examination, particular attention being paid to the lighter category repairs upon which a full report is made to the Progress Office. In the case of General and Intermediate Repairs, note is made of any major requirements.

The information obtained at the Reception Shop, in conjunction with the Outstation reports and shopping control recommendations, is used to make a daily allocation to the erecting Shops. These particulars are circulated to all Shops in the form of 'Daily Advices', which also give information regarding the boilers allocated.

In the Erecting Shops, the locomotives are allocated to 'circuits' appropriate to their size in which they are repaired progressively in four stages comprising stripping, frame rectification, first stage assembly and second stage assembly. The work to be done is determined by Initial Inspectors answerable to the Chief Progress Inspector, whose findings are collected by Progress Clerks and entered on pre-printed work

sheets. On these sheets are marked the dates by which each particular group of items is required, in accordance with standard schedules, the anticipated date for the completion of frame rectification being taken as zero. Four copies of the work sheets are made out, one of which is perforated so that each portion may be distributed to the appropriate Shop gang, the three other copies being retained intact by the Progress Office, the Erecting Shop and the repair Shop Office concerned. Provision is made on the forms for the certification of completed work by Shop Inspectors under the Foremen, but the forms are not chargeable wages documents and, from the particulars thereon, separate piecework certificates are made out by the Shop clerical staff for the payment of the artisan staff.

Once the engines are routed, the progress of work is supervised from the Progress Office by Inspectors who follow the engine moves to ensure that the scheduled dates are kept by anticipating and overcoming any delays to items under repair.

Ex-London, Midland & Scottish Railway

On receipt at the Works, every engine and tender is given a preliminary examination to confirm the information already supplied regarding the extent of the repairs involved, and to bring to light any items requiring particular attention. After this examination by an Initial Examiner, the Assistant to the Works Superintendent (Locomotive Maintenance) makes the final decision on the class of repair to be undertaken.

The Progress and Shopping Assistant, who is his assistant, in collaboration with the Chief Foreman of the Erecting Shop, determines daily the actual input of engines and tenders into the Erecting and Tender Shops where the Progressive Repair System is in operation. Under this system, the engines and tenders move along the repair lines by stages, each stage being confined to a particular group of repair operations. The entry of each engine and tender into the repair lines and the subsequent moves from stage to stage are made to a definite time schedule. From the schedule are derived supplementary time schedules by which components dismantled for repair in the various Shops are routed so as to be available at the appropriate time for reassembly on the engines and tenders.

By means of the 'Daily Minutes', all Shops and Offices are kept advised of a wide range of information relating to the locomotives being repaired, including the allocation of engines and tenders to the repair lines, boilers allocated to engines, particulars of items in short supply or delayed in repairing, and new or amended instructions relating to repair procedure.

Initial examination proceeds concurrently with dismantling, the Initial Examiners, who are answerable to the Progress and Shopping Assistant, determining the extent of the repair work and marking up the work-authorising schedules which are pre-printed documents giving full details of all possible operations. These schedules are the medium by which work is initiated and replacement materials requisitioned and, after the Finished Work Inspectors have endorsed them to show authorised work completed in a satisfactory manner, they are used as wages documents for the payment of the men concerned.

Liaison between the Erecting Shop and the Shops engaged in the repair of components is maintained by Progressmen who investigate shortages and pay particular attention to out-of-course work of an exceptional nature.

Progress boards are maintained by the staff of the Assistant to Works Superintendent (Locomotive Maintenance) so that all concerned may have a comprehensive picture of the position in regard to major components such as boilers and cylinders. Movements of all engines and tenders in the Works are recorded on a master progress board.

Progress sheets are used so that the Chargehands are fully informed of their commitments, and these sheets are entered up daily from information given in the 'Daily Minutes'. The sheets show, for each engine and tender, the day and time by which the repaired components must be returned to the Erecting Shop for refitting. One copy is prominently displayed in the Shop and one is retained by the Chargehand, each sheet being marked up currently as the work proceeds.

An analysis of engines repaired is produced weekly showing the time each engine has been on the Works, the time actually under repair, the time taken for testing and weighing and all other relevant information. In this way, there is a continuous check upon the efficiency of the repair arrangements and the overall time taken to deal with engines is kept at a minimum.

Ex-London & North Eastern Railway

The methods employed for progressing engine repairs vary considerably in detail at different Works. There is, however, substantial agreement on the principles.

On arrival in the Shops, engines are stripped and the parts cleaned and passed to the examination bench, when the work to be done is decided upon. The component parts are then sent to the repair Shops and new parts are ordered. The dates on which these components will be required in the Erecting Shop are established from schedules and advised to all concerned.

At each Works, one Assistant to the Works Manager, or Works Assistant, is responsible for the detailed scheduling procedure and he prepares weekly a programme showing the engines to be completed in the current week and in the two succeeding weeks. This three-weekly programme is drawn up at a meeting attended by the Chief Foremen and Progressmen. The availability of boilers and other major components is established at this meeting and any delays are reported and appropriate action agreed.

Progressing of components through the Shops is carried out by Progressmen responsible to the individual Shop Foremen, and progress boards are maintained in the principal production Shops to advise Chargemen of the dates on which parts are required in the Erecting Shop and to indicate progress made towards completion.

In general, efficient progressing of locomotive repairs in the ex-LNE Rly Shops rests more upon the close personal contact maintained between the Works Manager, his Assistant and the Foremen rather than upon a formal control system.

Ex-Southern Railway

Locomotives are received at the Works with a waybill indicating that they are being shopped either for a general overhaul or for an intermediate repair. In the case of the former no indication, other than the class of repair, is given of the work which may be necessary but, in the case of the latter, the waybill enumerates the specific repairs for which the engine has been sent in. These repairs have been previously agreed by the Chief Mechanical Engineer's Assistant for

Locomotive Repairs (Running Sheds) who has acted as Shopping Controller.

The work to be done is decided upon by the Foremen and Chargehands, the work on intermediate repairs being normally confined to that specified by the waybill, subject to other requirements which may be found during the course of the repair. Before any motion part leaves the Erecting Shop, however, it is inspected by Examining Fitters and only those parts requiring attention are passed forward to the Machine and Fitting Shops. Repairs to boilers and work involving the manufacturing Shops are decided upon by the Foremen concerned.

Engines receiving General Repairs are progressed to a definite schedule. All parts sent to other Shops by the Erecting Shop are dated for return and adherence to these dates is supervised by the Progress Office by means of schedules and Shop board cards.

Summary of Practices regarding the Control of the Progressing of Locomotive Repairs.

Broadly, the measures adopted for controlling the entry of locomotives into the Works are comparable, and the detail differences in procedure which exist arise largely from geographical considerations.

Independent examination of locomotives for the purpose of determining the degree of repair work necessary has been developed comprehensively only by the ex-GW and ex-LMS Rlys, and in the Works of these Companies the initiation of work-authorising documents is an integral part of the system of independent examination. In the ex-LNE Rly Shops, the determination of the repair work to be performed is dealt with by the appropriate Shop Foremen and Chargehands, assisted in isolated cases by wages grade artisan staff who, acting as Examiners, deal with particular items, eg cylinders and motion details. The use of pre-printed wages documents for this purpose is well developed, but the initiation of these documents is not independent of Shop supervision. Similar conditions apply in the case of the ex-Southern Rly Shops but, in addition, considerable reliance is placed, in the case of intermediate repairs, on the information given in the Shopping Proposal form.

The principles of progressive repair are applicable in varying degree at all the Works but only on the ex-GW and ex-LMS Rlys does this invariably mean the physical movement of the engine, tender or boiler from one repair stage to another in the Shop.

The use of time schedules to control the course of repair work is universal but, in the ex-Southern Rly Shops, this is applied only to General Repairs. The physical progress of components undergoing repair is dealt with in all the Works by Progressmen but whereas it is a feature of the systems used by the GW and LMS Rlys that, as in the case of initial examination, this control is independent of Shop supervision, in the ex-LNE Rly Shops, the Progressmen are directly responsible to the Shop Foremen.

The practices described are being modified to agree with the recommendations given in the Report of the Classification of Locomotive Repairs Policy Committee which have recently been approved by the Railway Executive.

General Particulars of the Main Locomotive Works – Great Western Railway

Reference No.	Works	Date Built	Railway Company, for which built	Total Area Acres	Covered Area. Acres	Percentage of Area Covered	Principal Activities	General Comments by the Committee
1	Swindon	1842	Great Western Railway	140.2	35.2	25.1%	Locomotive building and repairing. New boiler building. Laminated and coil springs for locomotives, carriages and wagons. Rolling mill for steel sections and bars. Iron and brass castings for entire Railway. Chair castings and points and crossing manufacture for Engineering Department. Outdoor Machinery maintenance (except Northern Division) and dock maintenance for entire Railway.	Although a 'square' works layout, has a reasonably direct flow from the manufacturing shops to the erecting shops. Two erecting shops with transverse layout.
2	Wolverhampton	1855	Great Western Railway	13.7	5.2	37.9%	Repairing all types of tank locomotives and the smaller tender locomotives. Outdoor machinery maintenance for the Northern Division.	There is a long Erecting Shop with external traverser one end and no wasted roof space. Machine Shop adjacent and parallel to Erecting Shop – excellent arrangement to reduce transport. If Boiler Shop, at present on other side of main line, could be moved over, this would be a very compact layout for repair work.
3	Caerphilly (Also performs carriage repairing.)	1899	Rhymney Railway	9.2	5.7	62.0%	Repairing tank locomotives of the types allocated to South Wales. Repairing items for South Wales Outstation Depots.	Very compact layout for locomotive repairs. Traverser Erecting Shop with covered traverser avenue. Position of ancillary shops good but could be improved by bringing together the two machine shops, thus facilitating supervision and transport.

London, Midland & Scottish Railway

Reference No.	Works	Date Built	Railway Company, for which built	Total Area Acres	Covered Area. Acres	Percentage of Area Covered	Principal Activities	General Comments by the Committee
4	Crewe	1843	Grand Junction Railway (later London & North Western Railway)	137.0	44.0	32.1%	Locomotive building and repairing. All new boilers for standard LMS Rly locomotives. Steel castings, drop stampings and heavy forgings for all LMS Rly works. Chair castings and points and crossing manufacture for Chief Civil Engineer's Department. Manufacture of signals, locking frames and crossing-gate work for Signal and Telegraph Department.	Very long works involving excessive internal transport and shunting. Closure of 'Old Works' and 'Deviation' would make a more compact works to control.
5	Derby	1840	North Midland Railway (later Midland Railway)	47.0	14.0	29.8%	Steam locomotive building and repairing. All diesel locomotive building and repairing for LMS Rly. Hot brass pressings for LMS Rly. Brass castings for Derby C.&W. Works. Chair castings for Chief Civil Engineer's Department. Works Training School for Apprentices.	Good central Machine Shop. Erecting Shop cramped considering size of works and repairs cannot be progressed straight through. Disadvantages of two levels in works with Wheel and Boiler Shops at lower level.

General Particulars of the Main Locomotive Works – London, Midland & Scottish Railway (Continued)

Reference No.	Works	Date Built	Railway Company for which built	Total Area Acres	Covered Area. Acres	Percentage of Area Covered	Principal Activities	General Comments by the Committee
6	Horwich	1887	Lancashire & Yorkshire Railway	81.0	17.0	21.0%	Locomotive building and repairing. Chair castings for Chief Civil Engineer's Department. Continuous casting plant for chairs and firebars in process of installation.	Long layout of works giving good flow of work and convenient arrangements for administration.
7	St. Rollox (Also performs carriage and wagon repairing.)	1856	Caledonian Railway	15.0	9.0	60.0%	Locomotive repairing. New boilers for ex-Scottish design engines only.	Compact layout for locomotive repairs with all main shops adjacent. Layout basically similar to Cowlairs.
8	Bow	1850	North London Railway	10.0	2.0	20.0%	Locomotive repairing chiefly for London, Tilbury and Southend Section. (Heavy boiler repairs at Derby.) Chain repairing and testing. Assistance with Outdoor Machinery in London area.	Very small works considering that general repairs are undertaken. Dependent on Derby for much assistance, especially with boiler repairs and wheels.
9	Kilmarnock	1858	Glasgow & South Western Railway	13.3	1.5	11.3%	Locomotive repairing. (Heavy boiler repairs at St Rollox.) Breaking up Scottish Division locomotives.	Present works smaller than the original one, much of which has been pulled down. Very small works to undertake general repairs.

London & North Eastern Railway

Reference No.	Works	Date Built	Railway Company for which built	Total Area Acres	Covered Area. Acres	Percentage of Area Covered	Principal Activities	General Comments by the Committee
10 (a) (b)	Darlington: North Road Stooperdale	1863 1911	North Eastern Railway	27.0 17.5 44.5	11.0 4.0 15.0	40.7% 22.9% 33.7%	Locomotive building and repairing. New boiler building. Area Outdoor Machinery maintenance.	Stooperdale Boiler Shop separate from North Road Works. Separate machine shops, one at a higher level. Difficult entry to Erecting Shop pits via turntable and crane.
11	Doncaster	1853	Great Northern Railway	61.0	13.0	21.3%	Locomotive building and repairing. New boiler building. All patternmaking for LNE Rly locomotive works. Area Outdoor Machinery maintenance.	Crimpsall Shops for engine repairs are separate from new building and manufacturing side of works. Otherwise a rather straggling layout. Room for expansion.
12	Gorton	1849	Manchester, Sheffield & Lincolnshire Railway (later Great Central Railway)	30.6	14.7	48.1%	Locomotive repairing. New boiler building. Cylinder castings for all LNE Rly works. Chair castings and points and crossings manufacture for Chief Civil Engineer's Department. Area Outdoor Machinery maintenance.	Layout constricted by surroundings and deficient in yard space. Boiler repairing dispersed around works and a progressive layout would be advantageous.
13	Cowlairs (Also performs carriage and wagon repairing)	1842	Edinburgh & Glasgow Railway (later North British Railway)	15.5	7.1	45.7%	Locomotive repairing. New boiler building. Mechanised casting plant for brake blocks and other repetition castings for all LNE Rly works. Area Outdoor Machinery maintenance.	Mechanised foundry of good design. Basic layout for works similar to St Rollox, giving very compact layout of shops, but restrictions on future expansion.

General Particulars of the Main Locomotive Works – London & North Eastern Railway (Continued)

Reference No.	Works	Date Built	Railway Company for which built	Total Area. Acres	Covered Area. Acres	Percentage of Area Covered	Principal Activities	General Comments by the Committee
14	Stratford	1847	Eastern Counties Railway (later Great Eastern Railway	31.2	11.5	36.8%	Locomotive repairing. New boiler building. Area Outdoor Machinery maintenance.	Inconvenient layout with shops broken up by main lines and running sheds. Excessive internal shunting and transport which inevitably must retard output. Entry into Erecting Shop restricted by size of turntable.
15	Inverurie (Also performs carriage and wagon repairing.)	1903	Great North of Scotland Railway	15.1	2.8	18.5%	Locomotive repairing. Area Outdoor Machinery maintenance.	Good straight layout. Excessive yard space with ample room for expansion, though northerly location does not merit such consideration. Erecting Shop crane needs renewal.

Southern Railway

Reference No.	Works	Date Built	Railway Company for which built	Total Area. Acres	Covered Area. Acres	Percentage of Area Covered	Principal Activities	General Comments by the Committee
16	Eastleigh	1909	London & South Western Railway	41.2	10.9	26.5%	Eastleigh and Ashford have much larger allocations of engine repairs than Brighton. Brighton also does engine repairs to assist the other works to meet their requirements and to balance variations in the new engine building arrangements.	Only four main buildings, giving perhaps the most compact of all the Main Works on the British Railways. Excellent direct flow of work from manufacturing shops through Machine Shop to Erecting Shop.
17	Ashford (Also performs wagon building and repairing.)	1847	South Eastern Railway (later South Eastern & Chatham Railway)	26.2	8.6	32.8%	All three works are capable of building new engines and boilers, but the manufacturing capacity of them all is 'pooled' for this purpose. Because of the existing allocation of repair responsibilities, the larger part of the new engine and new boiler assembly work available has been carried out at Brighton.	A long works in which the bays are too narrow in proportion to the length, giving excessive run of wall. The Erecting Shop combines long roads with short transverse pits served by a traverser and is the only composite example on British Railways.
18	Brighton	1840	London & Brighton Railway (later London, Brighton & South Coast Railway)	9.0	7.0	77.8%	Foundry and forge work for locomotives, carriages and wagons has been centralised at Eastleigh Locomotive Works as far as practicable, but drop stampings have been centralised in Eastleigh Carriage and Wagon Works.	A compact works with the highest proportion of covered accommodation. No room for further expansion. Recovery value of site small; no road access at present and provision economically impracticable.

Comparative Statement Showing the Main Division of Works Sections used by the Four Railway Companies at ... ...

Ex-G.W. Rly	Ex-L.M.S. Rly	Ex-L.N.E. Rly	Ex-Southern Rly
1. Swindon (i) Locomotive Maintenance and New Work, embracing (a) Initial inspection and progressing of repaired locomotives. (b) Material ordering and progressing of new locomotives. (c) Stock order control. (d) Repairs of components for Motive Power Dept. (ii) Estimating, embracing (a) Estimating and control of expenditure. (b) Piecework control. (iii) Plant Maintenance. (iv) Clerical (Staff and general). **2. Wolverhampton and** **3. Caerphilly** (i) Initial inspection and progressing. (ii) Repairs of components for Motive Power Dept. (iii) Drawing Office (Plant Maintenance) (iv) Clerical (Staff and general).	**4. Crewe** **5. Derby** **6. Horwich and** **7. St Rollox** (i) Production Planning, embracing (a) Process planning. (b) Estimating and control of expenditure. (c) Jig and tool design. (d) Material ordering and progressing for new locomotives and stock order work. (e) Rate fixing and piecework control. (ii) Locomotive Maintenance, embracing (a) Initial examination. (b) Scheduling and progressing repaired locomotives. (c) Repaired components for Motive Power Dept. (iii) Finished Work Inspection. (iv) General Duties. (v) Machinery and Plant Maintenance (vi) Works Metallurgy. (vii) Clerical (Staff and general). **8. Bow** (i) Ratefixing. (ii) Initial examination. (iii) Progressing. (iv) Clerical. **9. Kilmarnock** (i) Clerical.	**10. Darlington** (i) Scheduling and progressing repaired locomotives and repaired components for Motive Power Dept. (ii) Material ordering and progressing for new locomotives and stock order work including mechanised scheduling. (iii) Scheduling and progressing new and repaired boilers. (iv) Piecework control and new machinery schemes. *(v) Budgetary control. †(vi) Clerical (Staff and general). **11. Doncaster** (i) Scheduling and progressing repaired locomotives and repaired components for Motive Power Dept. (ii) Material ordering and progressing for new locomotives and stock order work (iii) New machinery schemes. *(iv) Budgetary control. †(v) Clerical (Staff and general). **12. Gorton and** **13. Cowlairs** (i) Scheduling and progressing repaired locomotives and repaired components for Motive Power Dept. (ii) Piecework control. *(iii) Budgetary control. †(iv) Clerical (Staff and general). **14. Stratford** (i) Scheduling and progressing repaired locomotives and repaired components for Motive Power Dept. *(ii) Budgetary control. †(iii) Clerical (Staff and general). **15. Inverurie** (i) Scheduling and progressing repaired locomotives and repaired components for Motive Power Dept. (ii) Clerical (Staff and general). NOTES: * Mechanical Engineer's staff. † Jointly by the staff of the Mechanical Engineer and the Works Manager.	**16. Eastleigh** (i) Scheduling and progressing new engine work and repairs, repairs of components for Motive Power Dept., and controlling stock order work. (ii) Jig and tool design. (iii) Metallurgical control. (iv) Clerical (Staff, estimating and general). **17. Ashford** (i) Progress and Jig and Tool, embracing (a) Progressing new engine work. (b) Progressing repaired locomotives and repairs of components for Motive Power Dept. (c) Jig and tool design. (d) Stock order control. (ii) Clerical (Staff, estimating and general). **18. Brighton** (i) Scheduling and progressing new engine work and repairs, repairs of components for Motive Power Dept. and controlling stock order work. (ii) Clerical (Staff, estimating and general).

Subsidiary Works

For the purposes of this Report the Subsidiary Works have been defined as those establishments at which classified repairs, other than general repairs, are carried out.

It has been evident to the Committee that there are considerable differences in policy in regard to these small Shops, the chief variations between the Railway Companies being summarised below:

GW Rly

The Subsidiary Works, by reason of their even geographical distribution throughout the Great Western territory have been used not only to save light mileage in working engines for the lighter classified repairs into the Main Works, but also as convenient centres for the maintenance of Outdoor Machinery within the Division concerned. Indeed, this latter class of work is usually of greater volume than locomotive repairs, and many of the staff are used for either duty according to the work available. It will also be appreciated that as the Divisional Superintendents control both Subsidiary Works and Running Sheds within their Division, they are able to relieve the Running Sheds of some unclassified repairs if capacity is available in the Subsidiary Works.

LMS Rly

The policy of the LMS Rly was towards the closing of smaller Works, and only four still remain out of ten. These are all under the direct control of a parent Main Works, and the staff is confined to carrying out classified locomotive repairs, except for slight machining assistance to Motive Power Depots in the vicinity. It can hardly be said that the locations of these Subsidiary Works do much to save light engine mileage except possibly in the case of Inverness, now in the Scottish Region.

LNE Rly

The Main Works of the LNE Rly are fairly evenly distributed along the route from Stratford in the South to Inverurie in the North, and this has lessened the need for Subsidiary Works. There is only Gateshead but this is a portion of a former Main Works which has been reopened to overcome the arrears of repairs.

Southern Rly

The Southern Rly has no Subsidiary Works in the accepted sense, but classified repairs are carried out by Running Shed staff at certain Sheds in the London area and along the former Western Section main line where steam traction still operates. At Bricklayers' Arms, New Cross Gate and Stewarts Lane only are there separate premises for this, but not separate staff. On the Eastern Section, outside London, Ashford is sufficiently centrally placed to deal with all classified repairs and few are required on the Central Section owing to electrification.

The actual results during 1947 should be regarded as exceptional, owing to the efforts being made to overtake arrears of repairs, because it is the policy to eliminate classified repairs at Running Sheds.

Classified Repairs at Subsidiary Works

The total average number of locomotives stopped at all the Subsidiary Works during 1947 for classified repairs only, is given below and, although the figure is small in all cases, it will be seen that, proportionately, a greater use is being made of these facilities by the two Railways on which the Running Sheds came under the direct jurisdiction of the Chief Mechanical Engineer, ie the GW and Southern Rlys:

Railway (1)	Average number of locomotives undergoing classified repairs in Subsidiary Works (2)	Total maintained locomotive stock (3)	Column (2) as a percentage of Column (3) (4)
G.W.	56.5	3,946	1.4%
L.M.S.	22.4	7,850	0.3%
L.N.E.	13.0	6,248	0.2%
Southern	24.1	1,877	1.3%
All Rlys	116.0	19,921	0.6%

It will be clear that the usefulness of the Subsidiary Works is dependent upon their ability to deal speedily with light classified repairs and so save the time and mileage involved by engines travelling to and from the Main Works, as well as relieving pit space there for heavier repairs. The problem is one of policy and equipment rather than of organisation, and could well be the subject of a separate enquiry to determine whether the Subsidiary Works are an economic proposition.

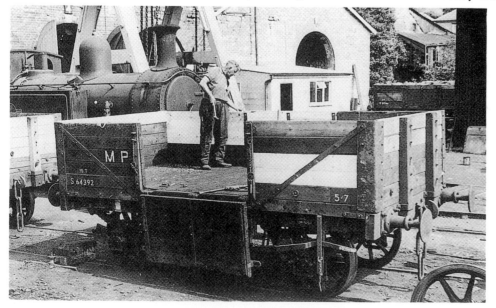

There were of course many small works throughout the system, undertaking local repairs. Here, an open wagon receives attention in the open at Ryde Works, Isle of Wight in July 1964.

(Peter Nicholson)

Particulars of Output during 1947 at the Subsidiary Locomotive Works

Works	Official responsible		Average No. of locomotives on Works	Classified Output		Other activities
	Designation	Location		Heavy	Light	
Ex-G.W. Rly						
Barry	Div. Loco. Supt.	Cardiff	10.5	9	115	Unclassified repairs.
Bristol, Bath Road	,,	Bristol	2.0	–	48	
Newport, Ebbw Jct.	,,	Newport	5.6	–	65	Divisional outdoor machinery maintenance.
Newton Abbot	,,	Newton Abbot	14.4	–	195	
Old Oak Common	,,	Old Oak Common	6.1	–	53	
Tyseley	,,	Wolverhampton	7.4	–	54	
Worcester	,,	Worcester	10.5	3	87	
Total			56.5	12	617	
Ex-L.M.S. Rly						
Bristol	Works Supt.	Derby	3	–	21	Nil
Inverness	Mechanical and Elec. Engineer	St Rollox	3.5	15	28	
Leeds	Works Supt.	Derby	5.6	5	108	
Rugby	Works Manager	Crewe	10.3	25	126	
Total			22.4	45	283	
Ex-L.N.E. Rly						
Gateshead	Works Manager	Darlington	13	–	238	Unclassified repairs. Grease factory. Outdoor machinery maintenance.
Ex-Southern Rly						
Bournemouth	Shed Foreman	Bournemouth	0.5	1	9	Unclassified running shed maintenance.
Bricklayers' Arms	,, Supt.	Bricklayers' Arms	4.8	9	28	
Eastleigh	,, ,,	Eastleigh	1.2	–	9	
Exmouth Jct.	,, ,,	Exmouth Jct.	1.3	1	5	
Feltham	,, Foreman	Feltham	0.9	–	4	
Guildford	,, ,,	Guildford	1.4	2	19	
Hither Green	,, ,,	Hither Green	0.9	–	4	
New Cross Gate	,, ,,	New Cross Gate	5.8	7	15	
Nine Elms	,, Supt.	Nine Elms	1.5	2	25	
Salisbury	,, Foreman	Salisbury	0.5	1	6	
Stewarts Lane	,, Supt.	Stewarts Lane	5.3	7	41	
Total			24.1	30	165	

British Railways Locomotive Works
Ashford Locomotive Works

Ashford Locomotive Works was built in 1847 on a 26½ acre site, by the South Eastern Railway Company. James I. Cudworth, Locomotive Superintendent at the time, designed and built a number of locomotives at the Works, including the 'Hastings' class 2-4-0s in 1853 and in 1861 the first of 16 express passenger locomotives with 7ft driving wheels. In 1899 the South Eastern Railway was amalgamated with the London, Chatham & Dover Railway and the Works was extended quite considerably shortly afterwards. H.S. Wainwright built 51 of the D class 4-4-0s during the period 1901 and 1907, one of which, BR No. 31574 is depicted.

In 1923 Ashford became part of the Southern Railway and continued in its role of repairing and constructing locomotives, and by the end of its era of locomotive building in 1962, when the work was transferred to Eastleigh, some 639 steam locomotives had been completed. After this date, Ashford built various items of rolling stock, including the 'Cartic' 4-articulated car transporter and continued to repair and build wagon stock for the UK and many contracts for overseas railways as far away as Kenya, the Middle East and Bangladesh.

Ashford Locomotive Works, Kent.
1846 February. Board of Directors of SER decided to purchase 185 acres on which to build a Locomotive Establishment.
1847 First construction works began and announcement made that in addition to the Locomotive Works a complete village would be built for the employees. Initially called Alfred Town.
1848 Construction of first locomotive commenced.
1853 First passenger locomotive completed – one of ten 2-4-0s.
1889 F class 4-4-0 No. 240 *Onward* awarded a gold medal at the Paris Exhibition.
1899 January 1st. SER amalgamated with LCDR to form SECR. About 409 locomotives built up to this time.
1900 Longhedge Works closed and locomotive work transferred to Ashford.
1911 Major rebuilding of Works completed after ten years of work.
1914 Ten L class 4-4-0s assembled by fitters from Borsig of Germany – locomotive order subcontracted by Beyer, Peacock.
1923 January 1st. SECR became the Eastern Section of the Southern Railway.
     Locomotives of the Eastern Section, under the care of the Works, received an 'A' prefix to their numbers.
1926 Royal visit by King George VI and Queen Elizabeth.
1937 First diesel locomotives built – three 0-6-0 shunters.
1941 Co-Co electric locomotive No. CC1 built.
1944 March. Last steam locomotive built – LMSR 8F 2-8-0 No. 8674.
1948 January 1st. Became part of BTC on Nationalisation. Wagon Works became separate from Locomotive Works.
1952 Last locomotive built – 0-6-0 diesel-electric shunter No 15236.
1954 Major rebuilding of SR 2-6-0s with new front ends, cylinders etc.
1962 Became part of BR Workshops Division.
     July. All locomotive work ceased and transferred to Eastleigh Works.
1992 May 30th/31st 1846 Erecting Shop, now used as BR's Heavy Repair Depot for cranes and on-track machines opened to the public as part of the Ashford 150 Railway Festival celebration.
     See also Wagon Works.

Aerial view of the Works in 1947 showing the Locomotive Works on the left, beyond the main line towards Folkestone, whilst the Wagon Works are on the right straddling the branch to Hastings.

(Southern Railway)

Construction of new South Eastern & Chatham Railway 0-6-0 engines in the early years of the Century.
(National Railway Museum)

A steam-driven traverser at Ashford made a fascinating sight in the loco-motive erecting shop in the early 20th Century during the Wainwright era.

(Southern Railway)

A 1919 view of the locomotive smithy was representative of this shop, which lasted into the British Rail ownership.

(Southern Railway)

The tyre furnace heated tyres to expand them so that the wheel centre could be lowered into position, thus creating a shrink-fit when cool, this was a sight common to all locomotive works throughout the age of steam.

(Southern Railway)

Ashford Works featured in a wartime "In Town Tonight" radio programme, during which a band played in front of Bulleid's Q1 class 0-6-0 'Austerity' engine, SR No. C26, just out of Ashford Paint Shop.

(Southern Railway)

Wainwright's D class 4-4-0s set a high standard of classical beauty. BR No. 31574 built at Ashford in 1907 was photographed in Ashford shed in 1955, painted in British Railways lined-out black livery. Fifty-one of the class were built between 1901 and 1907 by Ashford and outside contractors, 21 of them subsequently being rebuilt by Maunsell into D1s during the 1920s. These gained a good reputation on Kent Coast expresses with 28 of the un-rebuilt engines lasting into BR days, but all were withdrawn by the end of 1956. Wisely, one of the class was retained for preservation, restored to its original external condition and rich green livery, but not made fit to run.

(J. M. Jarvis)

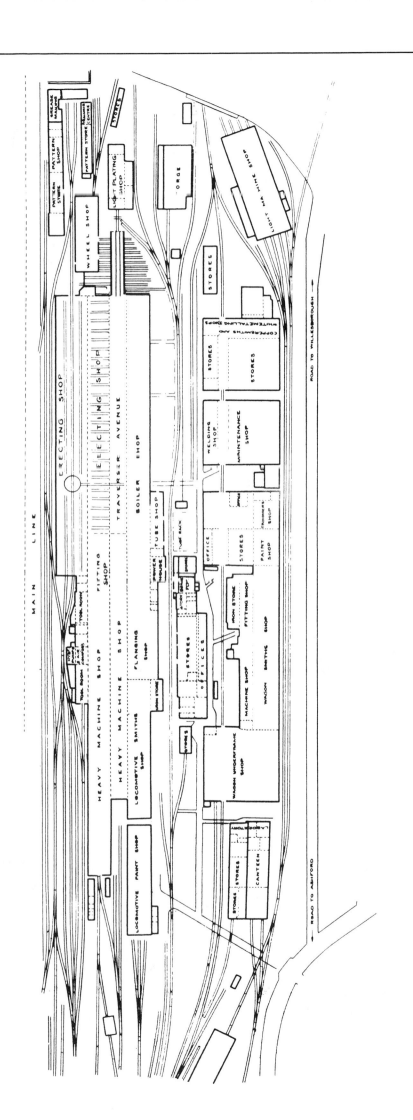

ASHFORD WORKS

(SOUTHERN REGION)

Bow Locomotive Works

Bow Locomotive Works was built in 1853 on a ten acre site, to service the City to Poplar Docks line, and at that time was owned by the North London Railway. Some time after 1918 the line was extended to Watford and during this period electrification came into force.

Under J.C. Park, the Works were rebuilt and enlarged to become one of the most advanced railway works in the British Isles, and in fact after 1860, all motive power was built here for the North London Railway.

Upon amalgamation into the LMS, Bow was still the smallest of the main works but its large, advanced repair shops were of inestimable value in the dock areas. In 1956, the steam sheds became the first all-diesel motive power depot on BR. At the height of its output, 750 men were employed here but upon closure in 1960, when all work was sent to Derby, there were but 150 men in employment.

Bow Locomotive Works, London.
1853 Workshops established for the NLR including carriage and wagons workshop occupying a total area of 31 acres.
1863 First locomotive completed – 4-4-0T No. 43.
1882 New erecting shop built.
1908 December. NLR came under the control of the LNWR.
1906 Last locomotive built – 4-4-0T No. 4.
1923 January 1st. Became part of the LMSR, continuing with locomotive repair work.
1948 January 1st. Became part of BTC on Nationalisation.
1960 Works closed and work transferred to Derby.

The Locomotive Superintendent's office as pictured in 1900 gave the impression of a museum, with its wealth of component samples, framed pictures and a fine model antique engine!

(National Railway Museum)

The wheel shop in 1898 makes a nice picture. Whilst the larger diameter wheel sets on view had presumably come off NLR 4-4-0 Tanks, the small pair of wheel sets in the right foreground, one of which had a crank axle, probably belonged to the ancient 0-4-2 crane tank, which acquired these 'H' sectioned spoked wheels in the course of re-building. The engine lasted another 53 years before withdrawal by British Railways.
(National Railway Museum)

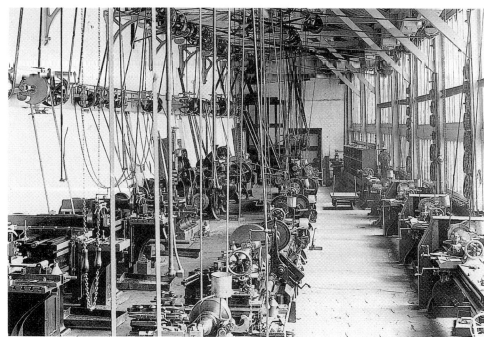

The machine shop at the turn of the century had a well lit and tidy appearance, so far as the conventional line shafting and belt drives permitted.
(National Railway Museum)

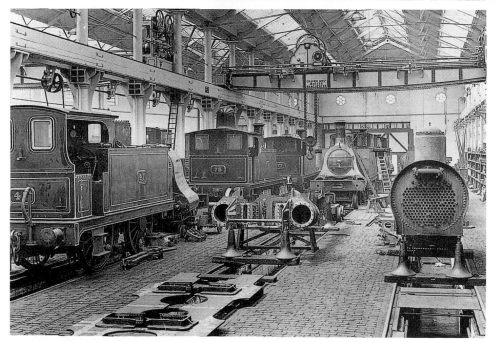

The erecting shop in 1898.
(National Railway Museum)

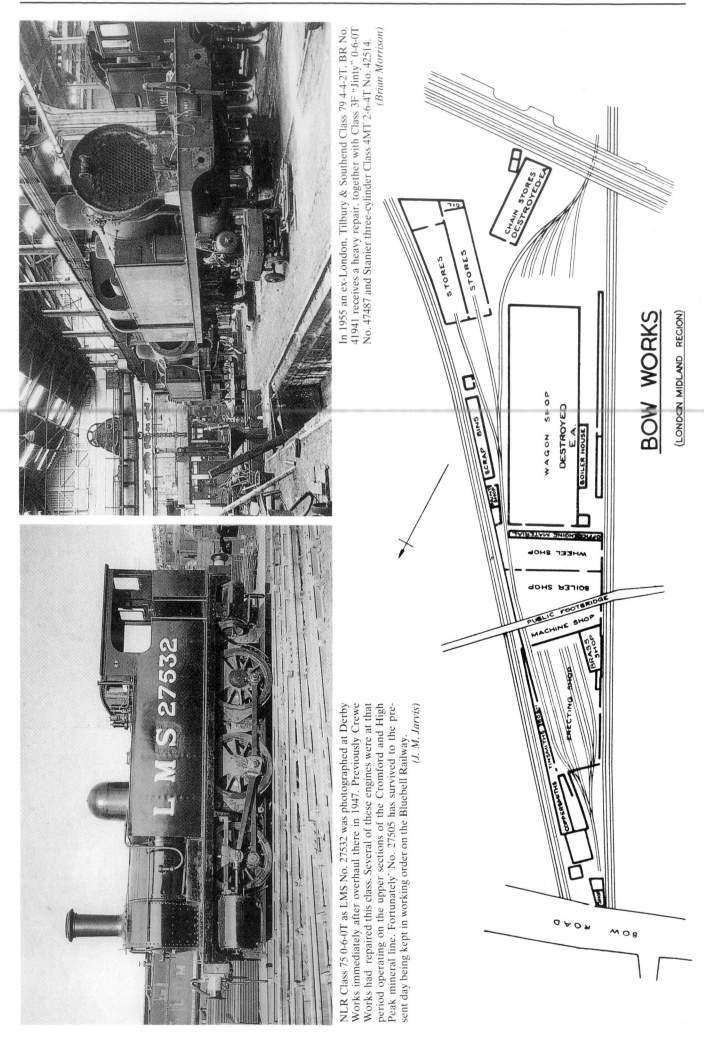

In 1955 an ex-London, Tilbury & Southend Class 79 4-4-2T, BR No. 41941 receives a heavy repair, together with Class 3F "Jinty" 0-6-0T No. 47487 and Stanier three-cylinder Class 4MT 2-6-4T No. 42514.
(Brian Morrison)

NLR Class 75 0-6-0T as LMS No. 27532 was photographed at Derby Works immediately after overhaul there in 1947. Previously Crewe Works had repaired this class. Several of these engines were at that period operating on the upper sections of the Cromford and High Peak mineral line. Fortunately No. 27505 has survived to the present day being kept in working order on the Bluebell Railway.
(J. M. Jarvis)

BOW ROAD

BOW WORKS
(LONDON MIDLAND REGION)

Brighton Locomotive Works

Brighton Locomotive Works was built in 1840 by the London & Brighton Railway, later to become the London, Brighton & South Coast Railway. It occupied a nine acre site next to Brighton railway station, and was heavily involved in the construction of locomotives, the first being built in 1852.

During the Second World War, Brighton Locomotive Works produced component parts for tanks and anti-aircraft defence along with the 2-8-0 freight locomotives which it supplied to the War Office at the incredible rate of one every 4.5 days.

Many different types of locomotive were constructed here, including the "Terrier" class 0-6-0Ts, the H2 class 4-4-2s as depicted, and finally the British Railways Standard 2-6-4Ts.

However, in 1964 the Works were closed, partly due to the restricted site area and difficult access, and the work was transferred to Ashford and Eastleigh. Since that date the site has been cleared and is now a car park serving the area.

Brighton Locomotive Works, Sussex.
1852 Established by LBSCR as their main works. First locomotive built was 2-2-2 No. 14.
1878 A1 class 0-6-0T No. 40 *Brighton* awarded a gold medal at the Paris Exhibition.
1889 0-4-2 No. 189 *Edward Blount* awarded a gold medal at the Paris Exhibition.
1923 January 1st. LBSCR became the Central Section of the Southern Railway. Locomotives under the care of this works received a 'B' prefix to their numbers.
1928 Ten U class 2-6-0s erected from parts supplied by Woolwich Arsenal.
1943 First of 93 Stanier 2-8-0s built for LMSR and LNER.
1948 January 1st. Became part of BTC on Nationalisation. 1,108 locomotives had been built up to this time.
Co-Co electric locomotive No. 20003 built.
1950 First Fairburn (LMSR) type 2-6-4Ts built.
1951 First BR Standard Class 4MT 2-6-4Ts built.
1957 March. Last locomotive built – BR 2-6-4T No. 80154, the 1,211 locomotive built.
Part of Works used for construction of BMW Isetta bubble cars – completed cars despatched by rail.
1954 1Co-Co1 diesel-electric locomotive No. 10203 built.
1958 End of locomotive work.
1962 Became part of BR Workshops Division.
1964 Works closed completely.

In 1954 ex-LBSCR class H2 4-4-2 BR No. 32421 *South Foreland* was being reassembled after its final heavy general repair. This engine was the first Atlantic type to be built at Brighton, in 1911 to Marsh's design, the earlier H1 Atlantic having been supplied by Kitson of Leeds. To the right of the picture is ex-LMS diesel-electric locomotive No. 10000 which was receiving attention, and in front of it is a new Standard 2-6-4T, No. 80094 under construction.

(Brian Morrison)

One of Brighton Works' famed 0-6-0T 'Terriers' – No. 32635 in LBSCR livery and appropriately lettered, seen at Brighton on 11th May 1961. Fifty of Stroudley's A1 Class – many later rebuilt as A1x – were built at Brighton and no less than ten survive today in preservation.

(Peter Nicholson)

No. 80010 was the first of the large, modern British Railways Standard 2-6-4Ts built at Brighton, in 1951. The Riddles 2-6-4T was a close derivative of the Fairburn tanks of the LMS, which were successors to the Stanier 2-6-4Ts, which in turn followed the Fowler parallel-boilered tanks. These various series operated very widely over the whole of the United Kingdom. Several of the British Railways Standard series have been preserved as well as some of the other taper boilered predecessors.

(J. M. Jarvis)

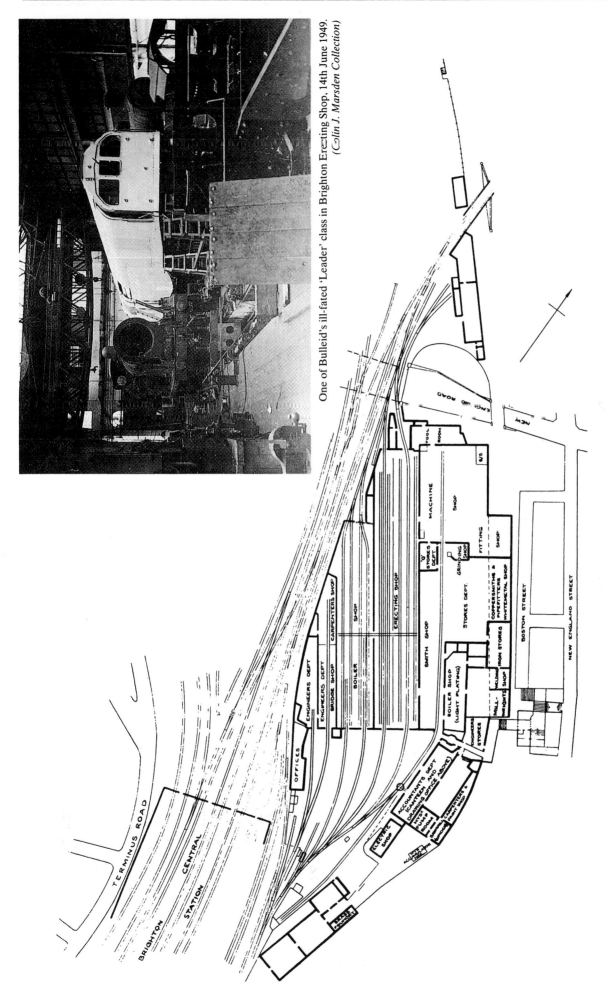

One of Bulleid's ill-fated 'Leader' class in Brighton Erecting Shop. 14th June 1949.
(Colin J. Marsden Collection)

BRIGHTON WORKS

(SOUTHERN REGION)

Caerphilly Locomotive Works

Caerphilly Locomotive Works was built in 1899 for the Rhymney Railway to replace the original workshops which were situated at Cardiff Docks. It was the only main works in Wales and served a 23-mile stretch of line from Rhymney to Cardiff. The site was a total of nine acres.

The Works did not actually construct locomotives, but undertook a considerable amount of repair work and also the modernisation and standardisation of existing locomotives. Up until 1922, only locomotives for Rhymney were repaired but after this date work began to come in from other railway companies and

the site was considerably expanded. In view of this, several other smaller works in Wales were closed and the work transferred to Caerphilly, although even at its peak only about 700 men were employed at any one time. After 1923 it came under the larger umbrella of the Great Western Railway.

The Works were closed on 29th June 1963 and were converted into the Harold Wilson Industrial Estate, but the original name lives on in the form of the Caerphilly Railway Society which has an interesting collection of locomotives and rolling stock within the vicinity of the former works.

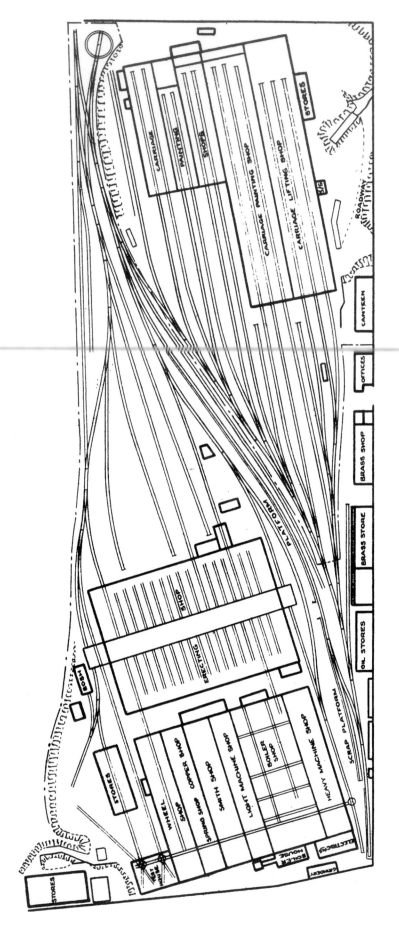

CAERPHILLY WORKS

(WESTERN REGION)

Cowlairs Locomotive Works

Cowlairs Locomotive Works was opened in 1842 for the Edinburgh & Glasgow Railway Company which was later amalgamated into the North British Railway. Although the site covered a total of 167 acres, access was difficult. It commenced building new locomotives in 1844 with the six-wheeled *Hercules*. However, construction was ended in 1923 after the amalgamation and only boilers were manufactured after that date. Cowlairs contributed to the war effort by constructing sections for Horsa gliders.

The Works employed a considerable number of staff, and in 1947 this totalled 2,475, but following Nationalisation much of the work was transferred to Horwich which was better equipped and by 1949 only 1,260 people were employed at Cowlairs. The Works were finally closed in 1968 and everything was then done at St Rollox Works.

Cowlairs Locomotive Works, Glasgow.
1841 Works built by the Edinburgh & Glasgow Railway, being one of the first railway owned locomotive workshops.
1842 Railway opened for traffic and works brought into operation.
1844 First two locomotives built – 0-6-0WTs for operation of Cowlairs Incline.
1865 E&GR became part of the NBR.
1866 Became main works for NBR.
1923 January 1st. NBR became part of the LNER. About 850 locomotives had been built up to this time.
1924 Last locomotives built – Reid Class N15 0-6-2Ts.
1948 Became part of BTC on Nationalisation, continuing with locomotive repair work.
1962 Became part of BR Workshops Division.
1968 Works closed and work transferred to St Rollox Works.

Cowlairs Works of the North British Railway started to build new engines in 1844 but ceased doing so in 1923, after the amalgamation into the LNER. LNER D31 class 4-4-0 No. 9769 (later re-numbered 2073) was built there in 1899, and was working on the former Great North of Scotland Railways' system in 1946, when it was photographed at Keith.

(J. M. Jarvis)

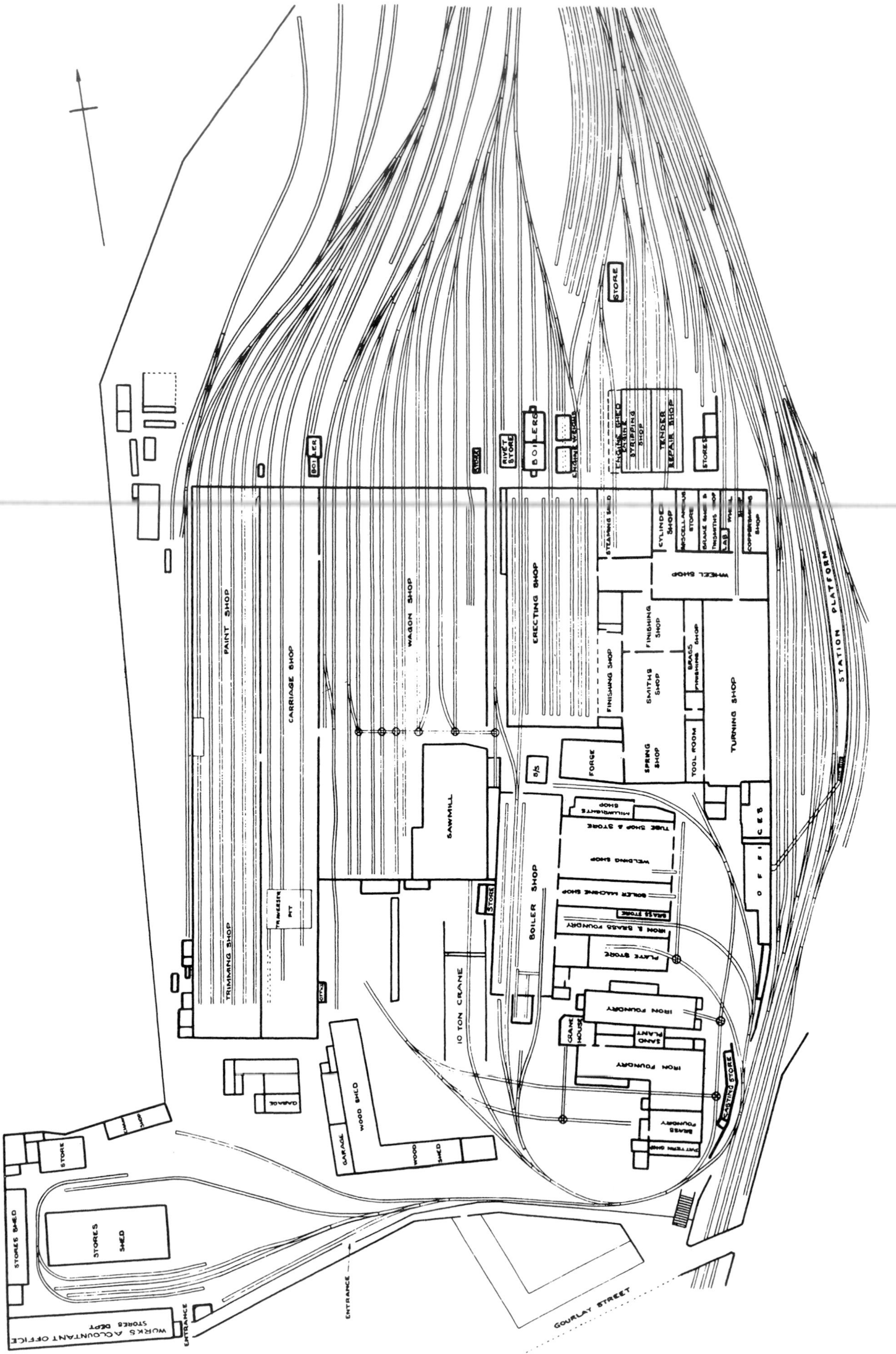

COWLAIRS WORKS

(SCOTTISH REGION)

PAINT SHOP

CARRIAGE SHOP

TRIMMING SHOP

TRAVERSER PIT

WAGON SHOP

SAWMILL

ERECTING SHOP

STEAMING SHED

FINISHING SHOP

SMITHS SHOP

FINISHING SHOP

BRASS FINISHING SHOP

CYLINDER SHOP

MISCELLANEOUS STORE

GREASE SHOP

TINSMITHS

LAB

COPPERSMITHS SHOP

WHEEL SHOP

SPRING SHOP

TOOL ROOM

TURNING SHOP

FORGE

S/S

BOILER SHOP

MILLWRIGHTS SHOP

TUBE SHOP & STORE

WELDING SHOP

BOILER MACHINE SHOP

BRASS STORE

IRON & BRASS FOUNDRY

PLATE STORE

IRON FOUNDRY

SAND PLANT

CRANE HOUSE

IRON FOUNDRY

BRASS FOUNDRY

PATTERN SHOP

CASTING STORE

OFFICES

STATION PLATFORM

BOILERS

CRANE WORKS

SHOCK

RIVER STORE

ENGINE SHED STRIPPING SHOP

TENDER REPAIR SHOP

STORES

STORE

STORE

10 TON CRANE

STORE

GARAGE

WOOD SHED

GARAGE

WOOD SHED

SHOP

STORE

STORES SHED

STORES SHED

WORKS ACCOUNTANT OFFICE

STORES DEPT

ENTRANCE

ENTRANCE

GOURLAY STREET

Crewe Locomotive Works

Crewe Locomotive Works was built in 1843 for the Grand Junction Railway, becoming part of the LNWR in 1846. The 137 acre site is in the fork of the main line to Liverpool and Scotland and the branch to Chester and Holyhead and was unique as the largest railway-owned works in the world. In 1843 it employed 161 men, but 100 years later in 1943 it employed approximately 8,587. It also incorporated its own 18 in gauge railway and employed a number of engines including *Billy* and *Dicky*, for transporting items around the main workshops. In 1886 the railway company built the gas works and later introduced the water supply from its own reservoirs to service the needs of the townsfolk. Their Majesties the late King George V and Queen Mary toured the works on 21st April 1913.

Following the formation of the London, Midland & Scottish Railway in 1923, a large plan of re-organisation was embarked upon to modernise the Works and make it far more efficient.

However, the first engine officially built at Crewe in 1845 was No. 49 *Columbine*. This engine was twice rebuilt and finally withdrawn from service in 1902 and preserved in the Railway Museum at York. Ten similar engines were built and were followed by the first of the famous "Crewe Goods", a 2-4-0 locomotive with 5 ft driving wheels. In 1858 Ramsbottom's 'Lady of the Lake' class, a 2-2-2, appeared. At the International Exhibition of 1862 No. 531 *Lady of the Lake* was awarded a gold medal and 60 of the class were built in

all, and two, *Marmion* and *Waverley* became famous in a race to Edinburgh in 1888. The first example of standardisation and mass production appeared at Crewe in 1858 in the shape of the 'DX' class which rendered more consistently good service than any other locomotive engaged on this type of duty and 943 were built at Crewe over the next 21 years. In 1862 Crewe became the locomotive centre of the LNWR, with all its wagon and carriage work being transferred to Earlestown and Wolverton respectively.

In 1923, Crewe Workshops, were amalgamated into the LMSR and Sir William Stanier was appointed as Chief Mechanical Engineer in 1932 which accelerated the onset of standardisation within the Railway. This resulted in a number of classes of earlier engines being made redundant and these were replaced by more standard types such as the 6 ft 2-cylinder 4-6-0 Mixed Traffic design and the 3-cylinder 4-6-0 Express Passenger engines.

During the Second World War, Crewe built 161 'Covenanter' Army tanks which were designed at Derby, as well as parts for heavy guns.

By 1947 Crewe maintained 2,779 locomotives whilst still being heavily involved in the construction of new engines. As construction of steam engines began to decline, Crewe continued its building programme with diesel-electric, diesel-hydraulic and electric locomotives, and even the HST (High Speed Trains).

Crewe Locomotive Works, Cheshire.
1840 Directors of the Grand Junction Railway decided to build a Locomotive Works at Crewe occupying a site of about three acres.
1843 March 10th. Transfer of work from Edge Hill Works officially completed.
  October, First locomotive completed – No. 32 *Tamerlane*.
  December 2nd. Completion of building the Works celebrated with a ball and banquet.
1845 July No. 49 *Columbine* completed – traditionally regarded as the first locomotive built at Crewe.
  GJR amalgamated with the Liverpool & Manchester Railway.
1846 GJR became part of the LNWR.
1862 Size of works extended considerably.
  May. *Tiny* completed – the first 18in gauge locomotive for the Works tramway system.
1864 Works further extended including opening of Bessemer steel plant.
1866 December. 1,000th locomotive completed – DX class 0-6-0 No. 613.
1870 Works extended again.
1876 August. 2,000th locomotive completed – Webb 2-4-0T No. 2233.
1887 June. 3,000th locomotive completed – 2-2-2-2 compound No. 600.
1888 0-6-0 No. 2153 assembled in 25½ hours – a world record.
1893 *Queen Empress* 2-2-2-2 compound awarded a gold medal at Chicago World's Fair.
1897 First locomotives constructed in the 'Steel Works' – 4-4-0s Nos 1501 and 1502. All previous locomotives had been built in the 'Old Works'.
1900 March. 4,000th locomotive completed – 'Jubilee' class 4-4-0 No. 1926 *La France*.
1903 No. 9 Erecting Shop completed at 'Steel Works' and 'Old Works' used for repairs only from then on.
1911 June. 5,000th locomotive completed – 'George the Fifth' class 4-4-0 No. 5000 *Coronation*.
1913 April 21st. Royal visit by King George V and Queen Mary.
1923 January 1st. LNWR became part of the LMSR.
1926 Works reorganised and No. 10 erecting shop built.
1930 Official 6,000th locomotive built – 2-6-0 No. 13178.
1937 June. First streamlined 'Princess Coronation' 4-6-2 built – No. 6220 *Coronation*.
1948 January 1st. Became part of BTC on Nationalisation.
1950 September. 7,000th locomotive built – Ivatt Class 2 2-6-2T No. 41272.
1951 First Standard class locomotive built for BR – 4-6-2 No. 70000 *Britannia*.
1957 First diesel locomotive built – 0-6-0 No. D3419.
1958 December. Last steam locomotive built at Crewe – 9F class 2-10-0 No. 92250. Officially 7,331st locomotive built.
1959 First main line diesel-electric locomotive built – Class 24 No. D5030.

1962 Became part of BR Workshops Division.
1964 Modernisation of Works commenced.
1965 All locomotive work at 'Old Works' ceased.
1967 Last Class 47 Co-Co diesel-electric completed – No. D1111, giving a total of 476 diesel-electric and 44 diesel-hydraulic loco-motives built at Crewe up to this time.
February 2nd. Last steam locomotive to be repaired – 'Britannia' class 4-6-2 No. 70013 *Oliver Cromwell*, bringing to an end locomotive work in the 'Deviation Works'. This was the 125,000th locomotive to be repaired.
1968 Completion of modernisation and reorganisation of Works.
1970 January 1st. Became British Rail Engineering Limited (BREL).
1972 New construction recommenced with building of prototype HST Power Cars.
1973 First of 36 Class 87 25kV electric locomotives built.
1976 First of 197 High Speed Train Power Cars – No. 43002, completed.
1978 January. 8,000th locomotive completed – HST Power Car No. 43081.
1983 First of 20 Class 56 diesel-electric locomotives completed – No. 56116.
1986 The only Class 89 Co-Co electric locomotive completed – No. 89001, later named *Avocet*.
1987 Construction of Class 90 electric locomotives commenced.
1988 First Class 91 electric locomotive built as a sub-contract for GEC Transportation Ltd.
1989 April. BREL privatised as BREL Limited.
1990 July 21st. 150th Anniversary Open Day.

This panorama of the brass finishing shop in 1906 shows the track of the internal railway system on the right hand side. The confusion of over-head shafting transmitting power by belts to the machines would now cause nightmares to Health and Safety Inspectors!

(National Railway Museum)

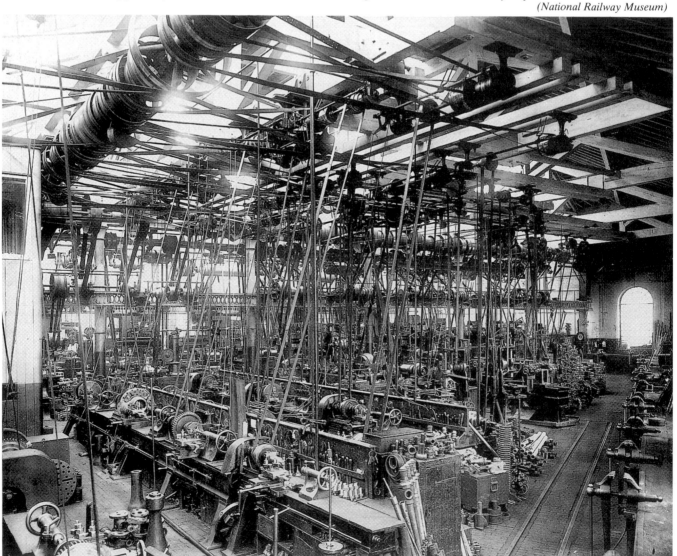

This boiler of a Webb four-cylinder 4-4-0 was having its firebox stays fitted in 1901 under the eagle eye of Chief Foreman Henry Cooper (1838-1911).
(Railway Technical Centre, Derby)

A new LMS Ivatt Class 2 2-6-0 being wheeled in 1947. 128 of these locomotives were built by several British Railways works up to 1953, to be followed by a further 65 British Railways Standard engines of almost identical design.

(LMSR)

The erecting shop around 1890, filled with engines of Webb's designs.
(British Railways)

Repair of electric traction motors at Crewe in 1975.

All the HST diesel power cars were assembled at Crewe in the 1970s and early 1980s. The High Speed Trains transformed the passenger services on various major routes, regularly running at speeds of 125 mph for much of their journeys. Each train has a power car at either end.

(British Railways)

No. 1876 – one of Alexander Allan's ten small firebox 6ft locomotives built in 1852 to the same design as *Columbine,* the first locomotive officially built at Crewe in 1845. After some rebuilding and the addition of a cab, *Columbine* was later retired in 1902, when fortunately it was preserved, and is now a valuable member of the National Collection. Allan's locomotives incorporated a distinctive outside frame, embracing the slide-bars and supporting cylinder, a feature that Allan continued on his new engines for the constituents of the Highland Railway from 1855-65.

(LMS)

LMS No. 6900 shunting at Bletchley in 1937. This was one of Webb's 80 5ft 5^1/$_2$in wheeled 0-6-2Ts built at Crewe from 1898-1902, incorporating Joy's valvegear. This engine became one of the last survivors of the class, and was renumbered 46900 in the British Railways series.

(J. M. Jarvis)

LNWR No. 2663 *George the Fifth,* the first of Bowen-Cooke's superheated 4-4-0s with 6ft 9in driving wheels, and Joy's valvegear. Ninety were built at Crewe between 1910 and 1915, and all carried names. Only three survived at Nationalisation, but were withdrawn the same year. This class was a development of Whale's 'Precursor' class 4-4-0s, of which 130 were built in 1904-7.

(LMSR)

LMS No. 5654 *Hood,* on shed at Rugby in 1937. This was one of Stanier's handsome three-cylinder 4-6-0 'Jubilee' class, of which 191 were built from 1934-36, and eventually were all named. With 6ft 9in driving wheels, they were designed for express passenger services. However, they were neither so numerous nor as successful as the smaller 'Black Fives' used for a wide range of traffic throughout the LMS system and beyond, and still built into British Railways days. *Hood* was one of 131 of its class built at Crewe, the remainder coming from Derby and the North British Locomotive Co. Fittingly several have been preserved in working order.

(J. M. Jarvis)

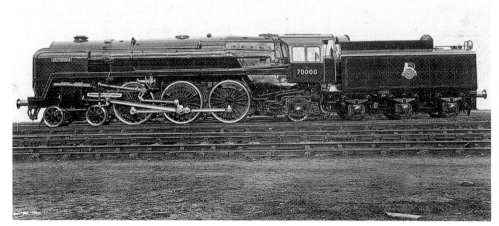

BR No. 70000 *Britannia.* Crewe built this British Railways Standard Class 7 4-6-2 with 6ft 2in driving wheels – the first of the BR series of twelve standard classes of steam locomotives. All, except the solitary Class 8 Pacific *Duke of Gloucester* incorporated only two outside cylinders, in order to simplify maintenance as well as construction. Fifty-five of the 'Britannia' class were built. This official photograph shows *Britannia* when new in 1951.

Crewe Works had its own extensive 18in narrow gauge system for transporting materials and components around and inside its various workshops. *Billy,* built at Crewe in 1876 was one of the fascinating diminutive engines, especially designed for this duty, to supplement the earlier engines which in the event outlived *Billy* and 'brother ' *Dickie.* The former incorporated some novel and highly advanced features, particularly for the boiler and valvegear. Perhaps Webb wanted to try out new ideas in the relatively secret environment of his main works? Various quaint old Allan type standard gauge engines appear in the background of the picture.

(LMS)

THE FIRST AND EACH THOUSANDTH LOCOMOTIVE
BUILT AT CREWE WORKS.
REPRODUCED TO THE SAME SCALE.

1845

1950

2000TH.   BUILT MAY 1876

L.& N.W.R. NO 2233.

2-4-0 4'-6" PASSENGER TANK.

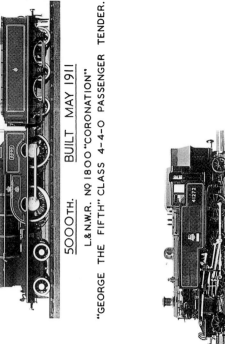

5000TH.   BUILT MAY 1911

L.& N.W.R. NO 1800 "CORONATION"

"GEORGE THE FIFTH" CLASS 4-4-0 PASSENGER TENDER.

7000TH.   BUILT SEP. 1950

B.R. NO 41272

CLASS 2 2-6-2 MIXED TRAFFIC TANK.

1000TH.   BUILT DEC. 1866

L.& N.W.R. NO 613.

DX. CLASS 0-6-0 GOODS TENDER.

PHOTOGRAPH SHOWS No 29 OF SAME CLASS.

4001TH.   BUILT MARCH 1900

L.& N.W.R. NO 1926 "LA FRANCE"

"JUBILEE" CLASS 4 CYL. COMPOUND 4-4-0 PASS. TENDER.

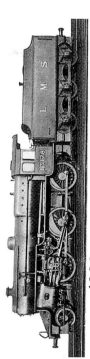

6000TH.   BUILT JUNE 1930

LM&SR. NO 13178   (NOW B.R. NO 42878)

CLASS 5 2-6-0 MIXED TRAFFIC TENDER.

1ST.   BUILT FEB. 1845

GRAND JUNCTION RLY. NO 49 "COLUMBINE."

"CREWE" TYPE 2-2-2 PASSENGER TENDER.

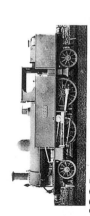

3000TH.   BUILT JULY 1887

L.& N.W.R. NO 600.

3 CYL. COMPOUND 2-2-2-2 PASS. TANK.

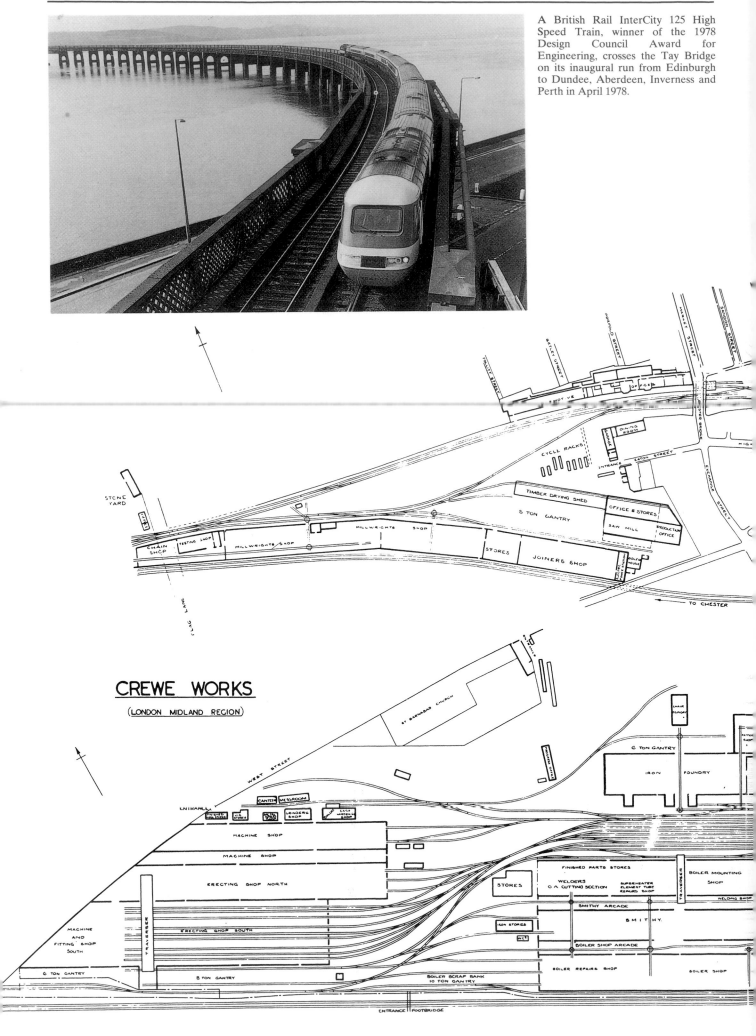

A British Rail InterCity 125 High Speed Train, winner of the 1978 Design Council Award for Engineering, crosses the Tay Bridge on its inaugural run from Edinburgh to Dundee, Aberdeen, Inverness and Perth in April 1978.

CREWE WORKS

(LONDON MIDLAND REGION)

CREWE DEVIATION & OLD WORKS

(LONDON MIDLAND REGION)

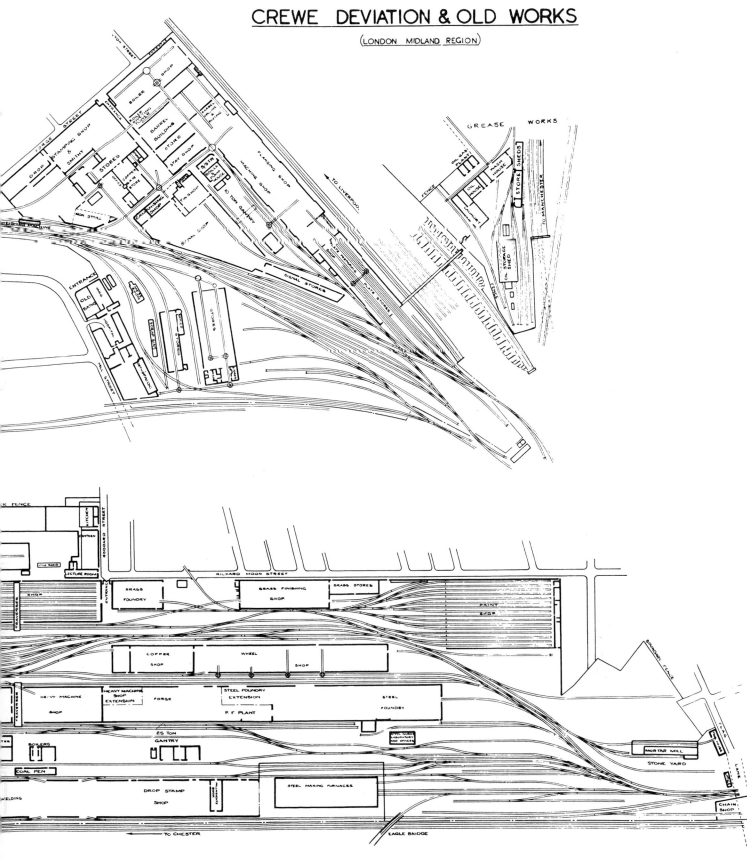

Darlington Locomotive Works

Darlington Locomotive Works was built in 1863 by the Stockton & Darlington Railway but this was soon amalgamated into the North Eastern Railway Company, and covered a site of 27 acres. At this time it employed a total of 150 men but this increased over the next sixty years to 2,760 and by 1954 reached an all time high of 3,815.

Darlington continued to build new steam locomotives at the Works and then in 1914 the first electric locomotive was constructed for the line from Shildon to Newport.

During the Second World War, Darlington manufactured 18-pounder shrapnel shells and a total of 1,064,554 were supplied along with many varied bombs and shells. After this period, however, and subsequent to Nationalisation, steam and diesel locomotives continued to be built. The last steam locomotive constructed here was completed in 1957 and the Works were finally closed in 1966.

Darlington Locomotive Works, County Durham
1863 Works completed by the S&DR.
      July. S&DR became part of the NER.
1864 October. First locomotive completed – 0-6-0 No. 175 *Contractor*.
1923 January 1st. NER became part of the LNER.
1948 January 1st. Became part of BTC on Nationalisation.
1949 First of 28 examples of Worsdell's J72 class 0-6-0T design of 1898 built for BR.
1950 First Ivatt, LMSR type 2-6-0s built.
1951 Last LNER/NER design locomotive built – J72 class 0-6-0T No. 69028.
1952 First BR Standard class locomotive built – Class 2 2-6-0 No. 78000.
      First 0-6-0 diesel-electric shunter built – No. 12103.
1957 June. Last steam locomotive built – BR Class 2 2-6-2T No. 84029 – the 2,269th steam locomotive built at the Works.
1962 Became part of BR Workshops Division.
1964 Last locomotive built – Class 25 Bo-Bo diesel-electric No. D7597.
1966 April 2nd. Works closed and site put up for sale.

0-6-0 No. 1557 is suspended by crane, and beyond a large gathering of workmen are gazing at the camera, presumably by request!
(National Railway Museum)

In the Gresley era, Stooperdale Boiler Shop contained an array of large boilers, with three near the front featuring the banjo domes carried by a large number of Pacifics.

(British Railways)

Darlington's Steam Hammer in Forge 1910.

(National Railway Museum)

The Machine Shop 1910 – large motors were used for a line of shafting. If a motor broke down all the machines were out of action. Nowadays each machine has its own motor of course.

(National Railway Museum)

The Erecting Shop, Darlington 1912.

(National Railway Museum)

Darlington Works continued to built new locomotives into British Railways days and produced the initial batch of Standard Class 2 2-6-0s of which No. 78000 was the first one in 1952.

(J. M. Jarvis)

In 1896 Darlington built this 0-4-4T, one of many used on local and branch line passenger trains by the NER and its successor the LNER. No. 7287 was one that had been transferred to Scotland, and was photographed in 1957 in Inverurie works yard.

(J. M. Jarvis)

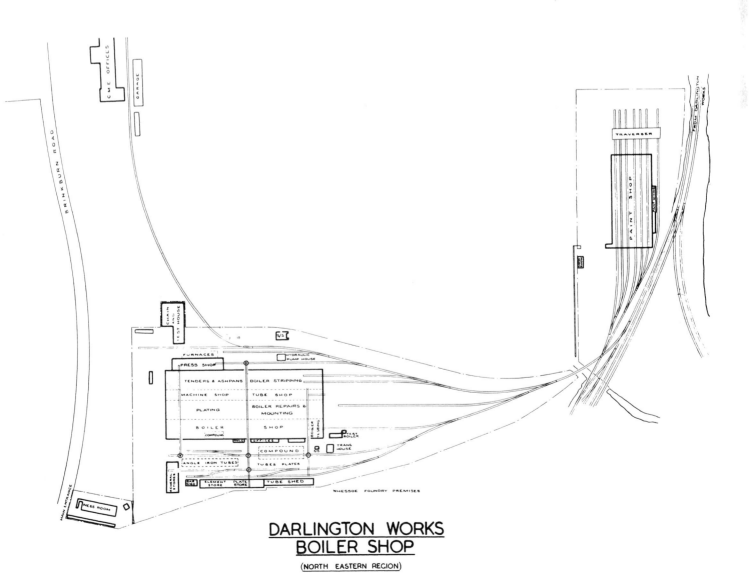

DARLINGTON WORKS
BOILER SHOP
(NORTH EASTERN REGION)

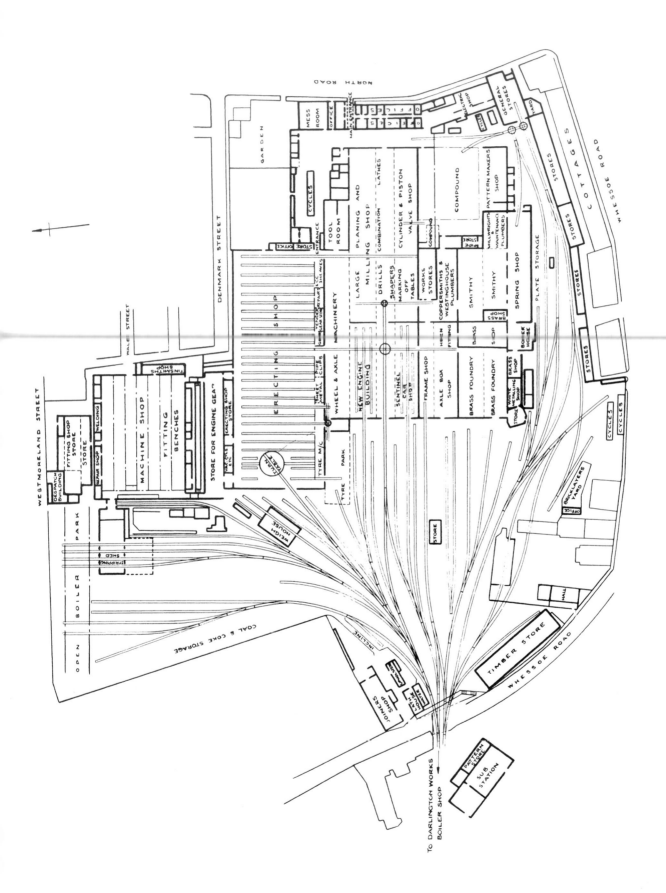

DARLINGTON WORKS

(NORTH EASTERN REGION)

Derby Locomotive Works

Derby Locomotive Works was built in 1840 by the North Midland Railway Company and eventually covered a total of 47 acres adjacent to the station. The Midland Railway continued to grow, linking Carlisle, Liverpool and Manchester to London, and further afield. Derby Works constructed its first new locomotive in 1851 and this was followed by many others including the famous Midland Compounds of which five were initially built at Derby in 1902/3 and a further 195 throughout the network. The initial locomotive, No. 1000 has been preserved at the National Railway Museum in York.

The last steam locomotive built, a 4-6-0 mixed traffic tender locomotive, made a total of 2,995 steam engines constructed at Derby. However, construction continued with diesel and diesel-electric locomotives until 1962 when such work was transferred to Crewe. In 1947 locomotives Nos 10000 and 10001, the first 1,600 hp main line diesel-electric locomotives in this country were built at Derby. By 1962, 3,500 members of staff were employed at Derby with a weekly wages bill of approximately £41,000. The Derby Works Training School was the first officially opened in 1947 by the LMS. Other staff facilities included the Works Canteen which could seat 960 people in one sitting, a hall with stage, complete with dressing rooms and a Works Surgery.

Derby Locomotive Works
1840 Works built by NMR for locomotive repairs.
1844 May 10th. NMR became part of MR.
1851 First locomotives built.
1873 Separate carriage and wagon workshops established.
1892 New erecting shop completed.
1923 January 1st. MR became part of the LMSR.
1934 First diesel locomotive built – 0-6-0 No. 1831.
1947 First main line diesel locomotive built – Co-Co No. 10000.
1948 January 1st. Became part of BTC on Nationalisation.
1951 April. First BR Standard class locomotive built – Class 5 4-6-0 No. 73000.
1952 Last LMSR type locomotive built – Class 2 2-6-2T No. 41329.
1957 June. Last steam locomotive built – BR Class 5 4-6-0 No. 73154.
1962 Became part of BR Workshops Division.
1967 Last diesel locomotive built – Class 25 Bo-Bo No. D7677.
1970 January 1st. Became part of British Rail Engineering Limited.
1973 Advanced Passenger Train – Experimental housed at Works for modifications during manning dispute.
1979 Six power cars built for the APT project.
1988 Classified repairs of diesel locomotives came to an end.

Building of 1,250 and 2,300hp Type 2 and Type 4 diesel-electric locomotives in Derby Works in 1959. *(BTC)*

Derby Dining Hall during meal-hour, opened in 1940 and capable of handling 1,000 men at one sitting.
(J. M. Jarvis)

This scene shows the apprentices working before the training schools were started by the Author.

(LMS)

LMS No. 10000 being assembled in Derby's 10A shop (formerly the paint shop) in 1947. This was the first mainline diesel-electric locomotive built in Great Britain.

View of the old No. 2 Erecting Shop towards the end of the 19th Century. This shop later became the electric shop, probably about 1910 when electricity was introduced into the works for shop plant and lighting. The picture shows that the limited space could obviously only accommodate 2-4-0, 0-6-0 and other small engines.

(National Railway Museum)

1980 Noble & Lund plano-milling machine. After fabrication, complete structures such as bogie frames required machining. The illustrated plano-miller has digital readout to assist the operator. A later machine had full CNC and a tooling carousel, and was the first BR machine to cost £1m.

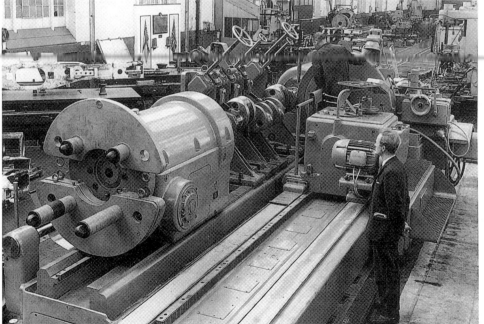

Left: Crankshaft grinding machines in Derby Locomotive Machine Shop in 1966.

(British Railways)

Below: LMS No. 13801 was one of the six 2-8-0s designed and built at Derby for the Somerset and Dorset line in 1914. It was photographed at Derby in 1947 after overhaul. It seems a pity that the Midland Railway, and also the LMS in its earlier years, did not acquire this sort of useful engine for the principal freight traffic, rather than perpetuate inside-cylindered 0-6-0 and 0-8-0 designs. Stanier's fine Class 8 2-8-0s began to make their mark from the mid-1930s.

(J. M. Jarvis)

Construction of Fowler 2-6-4Ts in LMS Derby Locomotive Works on 4th November 1933.

LMS No. 1013 was one of the famous Midland compounds, seen here stopping at Harpenden on a Bedford-St-Pancras train in 1938. Johnson built the initial five at Derby in 1902/3 to be followed by a further 40 in 1905/9 to a modified design by R. M. Deeley. Then the Johnson engines were superheated and rebuilt to conform to the Deeley series, which subsequently were also superheated. The LMS ordered a further 195 of the class from its own works and contractors, and operated them widely over its system. They were the only compounds to reach longevity in the United Kingdom, and all survived into British Railways days. The initial locomotive, No. 1000 has been preserved in the National Collection.

(J. M. Jarvis)

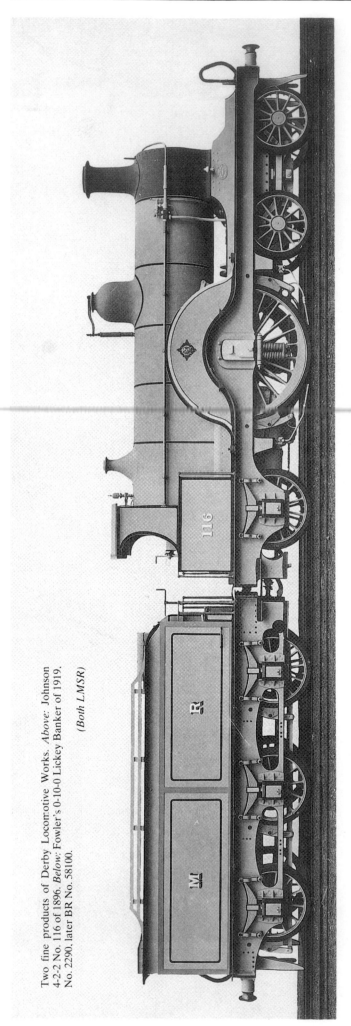

Two fine products of Derby Locomotive Works. *Above:* Johnson 4-2-2 No. 116 of 1896. *Below:* Fowler's 0-10-0 Lickey Banker of 1919. No. 2290, later BR No. 58100.

(Both LMSR)

DERBY WORKS
(LONDON MIDLAND REGION)

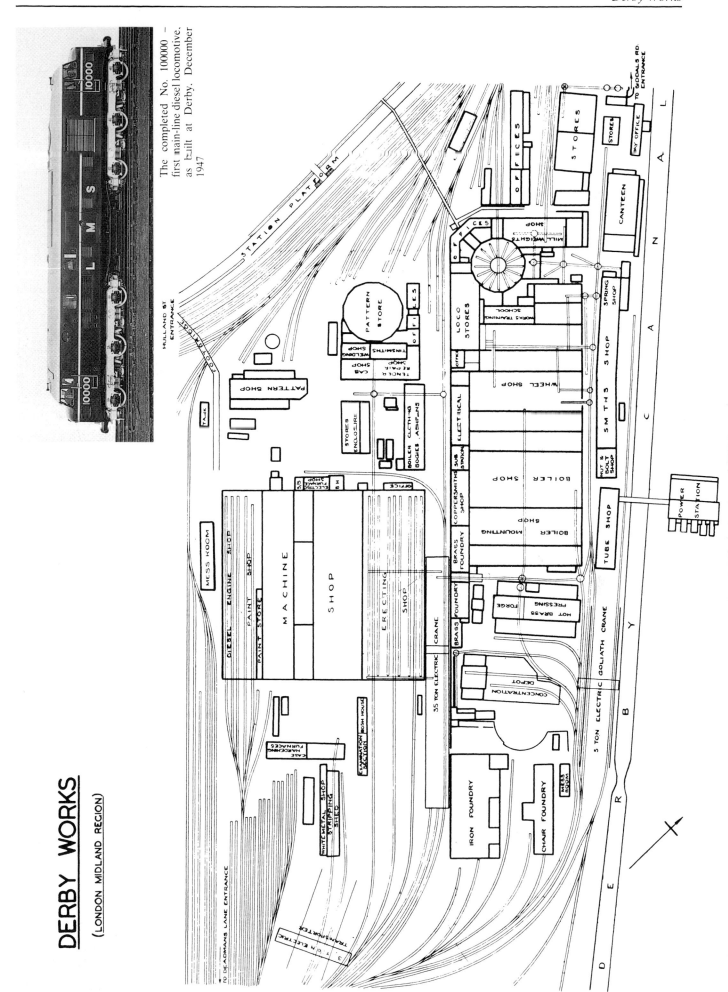

The completed No. 100000 – first main-line diesel locomotive, as built at Derby. December 1947

Doncaster Locomotive Works

Doncaster Locomotive Works was built in 1853 for the Great Northern Railway Company and covered a total site of 61 acres. It was known locally as "The Plant". New locomotives were not built there until 1866 when the existing sheds were extended on the instructions of Patrick Stirling, the Locomotive Superintendent. Many historically interesting locomotives were built at Doncaster, including Stirling's 8-foot "Single Wheeler" and the renowned Atlantics and Pacifics, the most famous of the latter being the Gresley streamlined *Mallard* which achieved the world speed record for steam traction of 126 miles per hour. The last steam locomotive built at Doncaster left the works in October 1957 and subsequently diesel-mechanical, diesel-electric and 25kV ac electric locomotives were built. Also, the 50 BR Class 58 diesel-electric freight locomotives of 3,300 hp were constructed here in the 1980s. During the Second World War, tank hulls and anti-aircraft projectiles were constructed at Doncaster.

From the period of re-organisation in 1962, all construction work was transferred to Doncaster from Stratford and Gorton. At this time, the total number of staff at Doncaster was approximately 3,600. Since 1986 the site has been BR's national locomotive stores in addition to undertaking the repair of diesel locomotives.

Doncaster Locomotive Works, Yorkshire. 'The Plant'

1853 Works completed for GNR.
1865 Erecting Shop and Boiler Shop extended.
1867 First locomotives completed – Stirling 0-4-2s.
1923 January 1st. GNR became part of the LNER.
1938 A4 class 4-6-2 No. 4468 *Mallard* completed – ultimate holder of the world speed record for steam traction at 126mph.
1941 First electric locomotive built – 1,500v dc No. 6000 (later BR No. 26000 *Tommy*).
1944 First diesel locomotives built – 0-6-0s Nos 8000–8003.
1948 January 1st. Became part of BTC on Nationalisation.
1949 Last LNER design locomotive built – A1 class 4-6-2 No. 60162 (later named *Saint Johnstoun*).
1952 First BR Standard locomotive built – Class 4 2-6-0 No. 76020.
1957 October. The last steam locomotive built – BR Standard Class 4 2-6-0 No. 76114; the 2,223rd steam locomotive built at Doncaster.
1962 Became part of BR Workshops Division.
1970 January 1st. Became part of British Rail Engineering Limited.
1974 Built Bo-Bo battery/rail electric locomotives for London Transport – Nos L44–L54.
1977 First main line diesel locomotive built – Class 56 Co-Co No. 56031.
1987 Last locomotive built – Class 58 Co-Co No. 58050.
     April. Became part of British Rail Maintenance Limited as a Level 5 depot. The dmu repair building became the Railpart National Stores Centre.

Crimpsall Erecting Shops about 1948 with Gresley Pacifics in the foreground including A3 class No. 60075 *St. Frusquin*.

(British Railways)

Great Northern Railway No. 1630 was Gresley's first locomotive design. This build (later LNER Class K1) comprised ten two-cylinder 2-6-0 mixed traffic engines built at Doncaster in 1912. A year later the larger boilered (K2) class started to appear, 65 of these being built. It was after he had subsequently built some two-cylindered 2-8-0s, and then some three-cylindered equivalents that Gresley was so impressed by the improved riding and performance of the latter, that he henceforth concentrated on three-cylindered designs. The valves of the inside cylinder valves were operated by his renowned conjugating levers from the two sets of outside gear.

(LNER)

GNR No. 1470 *Great Northern* was the first of Gresley's remarkable 4-6-2 express passenger engines. Two were built at Doncaster in 1922 prior to amalgamation into the LNER, for which he provided so many more Pacifics, including the streamlined A4s in the mid-1930s. No. 1470 had the largest boiler practicable, combined with a wide firebox, combustion chamber and large grate. The engine had three cylinders and con-jugated valvegear. However, *Great Northern* (by then No. 4470) was rebuilt in 1945 by Thompson with a different location of the three cylinders, each having a separate Walschaerts valvegear. Sister engine No. 4472, the famous *Flying Scotsman* has been preserved in working order.

(LNER)

Assembly of new Class 85 ac electric locomotives in the erecting shop in 1961. Forty of this class were built here, all with electrical equipment supplied by AEI, who by then had incorporated BTH, the original company involved. AEI was later absorbed by GEC.

(British Railways)

The elaborate underframes for the Class 86 electric locomotives were welded up in the fabrication shop.

Diesel engines undergoing thorough overhaul in the Crimpsall shops in 1970.

BREL Doncaster built the 50 Class 58 Co-Co diesel-electric freight locomotives of 3,300 hp, for BR. Whilst these had full width cabs at each end, the housing between covering the equipment was narrower, and unlike most of the previous designs it was not a load-carrying structure. As in the case of the original LMS Nos 10000 and 10001, the underframe itself was designed to support the entire load. (Shown here is the first of the class, No. 58001, when new in 1983).

(British Rail)

New wheel press in operation pressing a tyred wheel centre on to an axle of a diesel-electric locomotive.

Several of the 22 famous English Electric 'Deltics' receiving attention in the locomotive repair shop. These Class 55 locomotives were each powered by two Napier Deltic 1,650 hp high-speed engines. The class hauled the majority of the East Coast Main Line express trains from 1961/2 to 1981, when they were displaced by the new HSTs.

The Fabrication Shop at Doncaster Locomotive Works showing the manufacture of bridge beams for a BREL client in 1971.

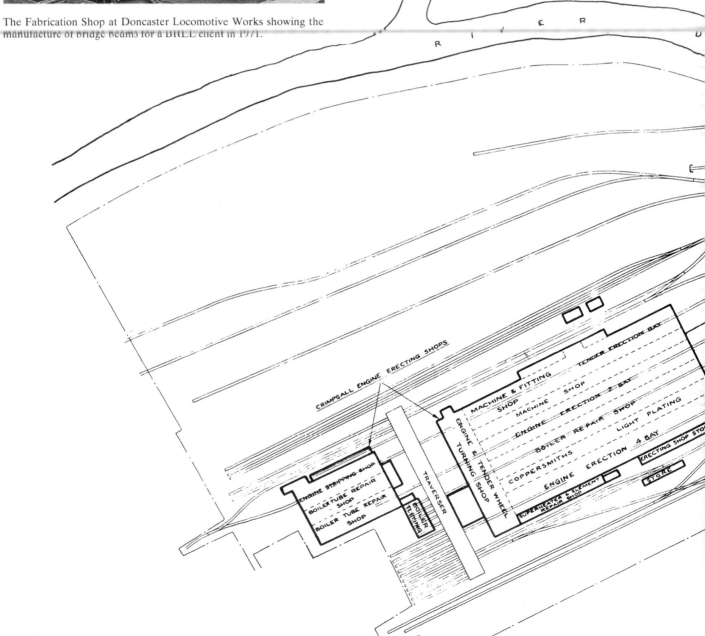

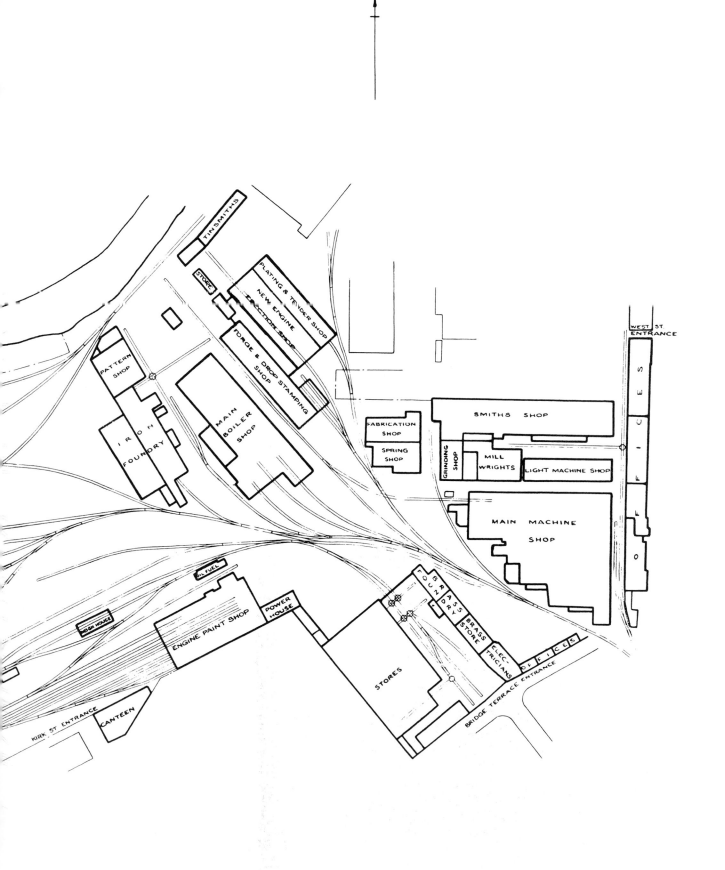

DONCASTER WORKS

(EASTERN REGION)

Eastleigh Locomotive Works

Eastleigh Locomotive Works was built in 1909 by the London & South Western Railway Company and covered a total area of 41 acres. In 1912 the first Drummond 465 class locomotives were built here.

Some notably successful classes of locomotive built at Eastleigh were Maunsell's 'Lord Nelsons', the 'Schools' class, Bulleid's 'Merchant Navy' class 4-6-2s, and LMS 2-8-0s. During the war years Eastleigh constructed anti-aircraft guns, assault craft and several types of steel-hull boats.

In 1962 Ashford locomotive repair work was transferred to Eastleigh, making the Works responsible for repair of steam, diesel and electric locomotives for the entire Southern Region, as well as repair of engines from multiple unit stock. However, all new construction was then ceased. In 1968 the Carriage and Wagon Works was amalgamated into the site of the Locomotive Works. By 1969, 2,788 members of staff were employed at Eastleigh. The Works is currently engaged in the repair of locomotives.

Eastleigh Locomotive Works, Hampshire.

1910 Works completed for the LSWR and first locomotives built – two S14 class 0-4-0Ts.
1923 January 1st. LSWR became the Western Section of the Southern Railway. Locomotives under the care of this works received an 'E' prefix to their numbers. 304 steam locomotives built up to this time.
1948 January 1st. Became part of BTC on Nationalisation.
1950 Last locomotive built – WC class 4-6-2 No. 34104 *Bere Alston*.
1956 First Bulleid Pacific rebuilt – MN class 4-6-2 No. 35018 *British India Line*.
1961 Last Bulleid Pacific to be rebuilt – WC class 4-6-2 No. 34104 *Bere Alston*.
1962 Became part of BR Workshops Division taking on all locomotive repair work for the Southern Region.
1968 Major modernisation and reorganisation of Works.
1970 January 1st. Became part of British Rail Engineering Limited.
1987 April. Became part of British Rail Maintenance Limited as a Level 5 depot.
(See also Eastleigh Carriage & Wagon Works.)

The Works Manager's offices on the right and the Erecting Shop on the left, background c1911. The LSWR had then only recently opened these locomotive works to replace those at Nine Elms, London, and thenceforth construction of new engines as well as repairs were carried out at Eastleigh. The office block remained substantially the same externally into the BREL era.

(National Railway Museum)

Iron foundry scenes, such as these moulds being prepared in 1911, remained typical of what could be seen at most main works into the middle of the 20th Century.
(National Railway Museum)

The machine shop when the works were new in 1910. The various machines were all belt-driven by line-shafts, in accordance with conventional practice of the time.
(National Railway Museum)

The new automatically controlled capstan lathes of the late 1960s provided an interesting contrast to the 1910 image, not to mention a much cleaner and tidier working environment.

(BREL)

Amongst the earliest engines built at Eastleigh were the ten D15 class 4-4-0s, which were D. Drummond's last design, as he died before the class was all built. BR No. 30469, pictured at Fratton in 1950, was built at Eastleigh in 1912, but subsequently acquired a Urie boiler. They proved to be one of Drummond's most successful engines, and for a period handled most of the Portsmouth expresses.

(J. M. Jarvis)

Lord Nelson, SR No. 850 was the first of Maunsell's 16 handsome and powerful 4-6-0s built at Eastleigh from 1926-29. They were the SR's largest express passenger locomotives until Bulleid's 'Merchant Navy' class 4-6-2s started to appear in 1941. Fortunately this splendid engine has been preserved in the National Collection.

Canadian Pacific was the fifth of Bulleid's large 'Merchant Navy' 4-6-2s and came out of Eastleigh in 1941 during World War I. BR No. 35005 was photographed in 1950 at Rugby when it was undergoing dynamometer car trails to establish the worth of the mechanical stoker which had been experimentally fitted. There were 30 members of this class, which incorporated various novel features, including a chain-driven valvegear enclosed in an oil bath. The large boiler with a steel firebox was an exceptionally good provider of steam. In BR days all the class were rebuilt into more conventional engines, appearance included, when their-magnificent power potential was combined with greater reliability. Bulleid also produced a more numerous class of slightly smaller Pacifics known as 'West Country'/'Battle of Britain' class, and these were able to operate over a much higher proportion of the Southern Railway's system. A total of 110 were built, mostly at Brighton, but six were completed at Eastleigh. Sixty of the class were rebuilt on similar lines to the 'Merchant Navy' class.

(J. M. Jarvis)

In 1968 the Locomotive Works and C&W Works were amalgamated on the site of the former Locomotive Works. The wheel shop, designed on a flow-line basis, was equipped for wheel and axle turning, tyre boring, assembly and balancing of both carriage and diesel and electric locomotive wheel sets. Assembly of roller bearing axleboxes and ultrasonic testing of axles also being undertaken.

(BREL)

The erecting shop by the late 1960s was involved in overhauling diesel-electric, electric and electro-diesel locomotives. Being wheeled is a Class 74 electro-diesel, converted from a Class 71 dc electric locomotive, and beyond it is a Class 33 diesel-electric locomotive, No. D6545 built by BRC&W Company.

(British Railways)

The diesel shop was specially laid out for expeditiously cleaning, stripping and overhauling the various types of diesel engines used in the locomotives and multiple units allocated to Eastleigh for repairs. Note the individual lifting equipment to facilitate the hoisting of pistons, etc. The shop also overhauled fuel injectors, turbochargers, exhausters and radiators.

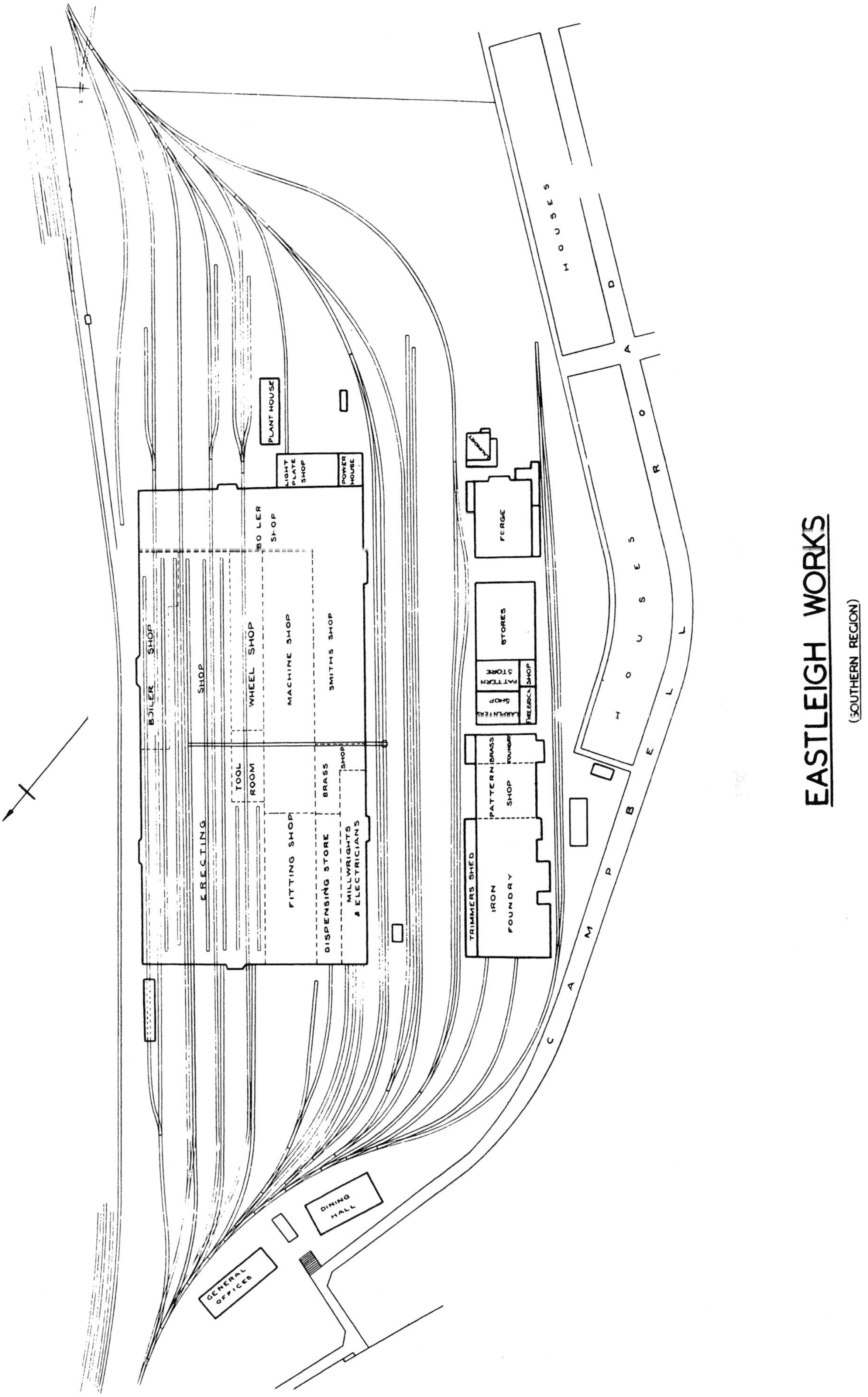

EASTLEIGH WORKS

(SOUTHERN REGION)

GENERAL OFFICES

DINING HALL

TRIMMERS SHED

IRON FOUNDRY

PATTERN SHOP

BRASS FOUNDRY

CARPENTER SHOP

PATTERN STORE

LABOUR STORE

STORES

FORGE

CAMPBELL ROAD

HOUSES

HOUSES

HOUSES

ERECTING SHOP

BOILER SHOP

TOOL ROOM

WHEEL SHOP

FITTING SHOP

DISPENSING STORE

BRASS

MILLWRIGHTS & ELECTRICIANS

SHOP

MACHINE SHOP

SMITHS SHOP

BOILER SHOP

LIGHT PLATE SHOP

POWER HOUSE

PLANT HOUSE

Gorton Locomotive Works

Gorton Locomotive Works was built in 1848 for the Manchester, Sheffield & Lincolnshire Railway Company and covered a total area of 30 acres. Some of the Gresley designed 'Director' class were constructed at Gorton in 1919.

During the First World War Gorton built some of the 600 2-8-0 freight locomotives for the War Department Railway Operating Division, the remainder being built by outside contractors. The Works carried out locomotive repairs and a variety of new parts manufacture. However, during the 1950s they made mechanical parts for, and then assembled, 64 electric locomotives. These were Co-Co passenger locomotive and Bo-Bo freight locomotives. At this time there was a total of 2,724 members of staff.

However, in the 1962 re-organisation, Gorton was closed and all work went to Doncaster. A supermarket now stands on the site.

Gorton Locomotive Works, Manchester. 'The Tank'
1848 Works completed for the MSLR.
1858 March. First locomotive built – 0-6-0 No. 6 *Archimedes*.
1897 August 1st. Railway retitled Great Central Railway.
1910 Works extended following transfer of carriage and wagon works to new works at Dukinfield.
1923 January 1st. GCR became part of the LNER. 921 locomotive had been built up to this time.
1948 January 1st. Became part of BTC on Nationalisation.
1950 Last steam locomotive built – B1 class 4-6-0 No. 61349, the 1,006th to be completed at Gorton.
     First 1,500v dc electric locomotive built – No. 26001.
1954 Last of 64 1,500v dc electric locomotives completed – No. 27006.
1962 Works closed as part of reorganisation and formation of BR Workshops Division.

The works carried out the repairs to the fleet of electric locomotives previously built for the Manchester, Sheffield and Wath line, as illustrated in this view of the electric traction repair and erecting shop, until the works finally closed in 1963.

(British Railways)

Fitting boiler stays to a locomotive boiler at Gorton Works in the 1930s.

(National Railway Museum)

Gorton's main shop c1936.

(Colin J. Marsden Collection)

GCR No. 506 *Butler Henderson,* built at Gorton in 1919 was latterly restored to working order and painted in its original splendid rich green livery and based for a while at Loughborough on the preserved Great Central Railway returning to the NRM at York in 1992. This official photograph was taken at Romiley in 1961. The 'Improved Director' class was so effective that Gresley built more for the LNER.

(British Railways)

LNER A5 class No. 5046 was one of Robinson's 43 4-6-2 tank engines built between 1911 and 1923 for the railway's outer London suburban service. It was photographed at Neasden in 1939.

(J. M. Jarvis)

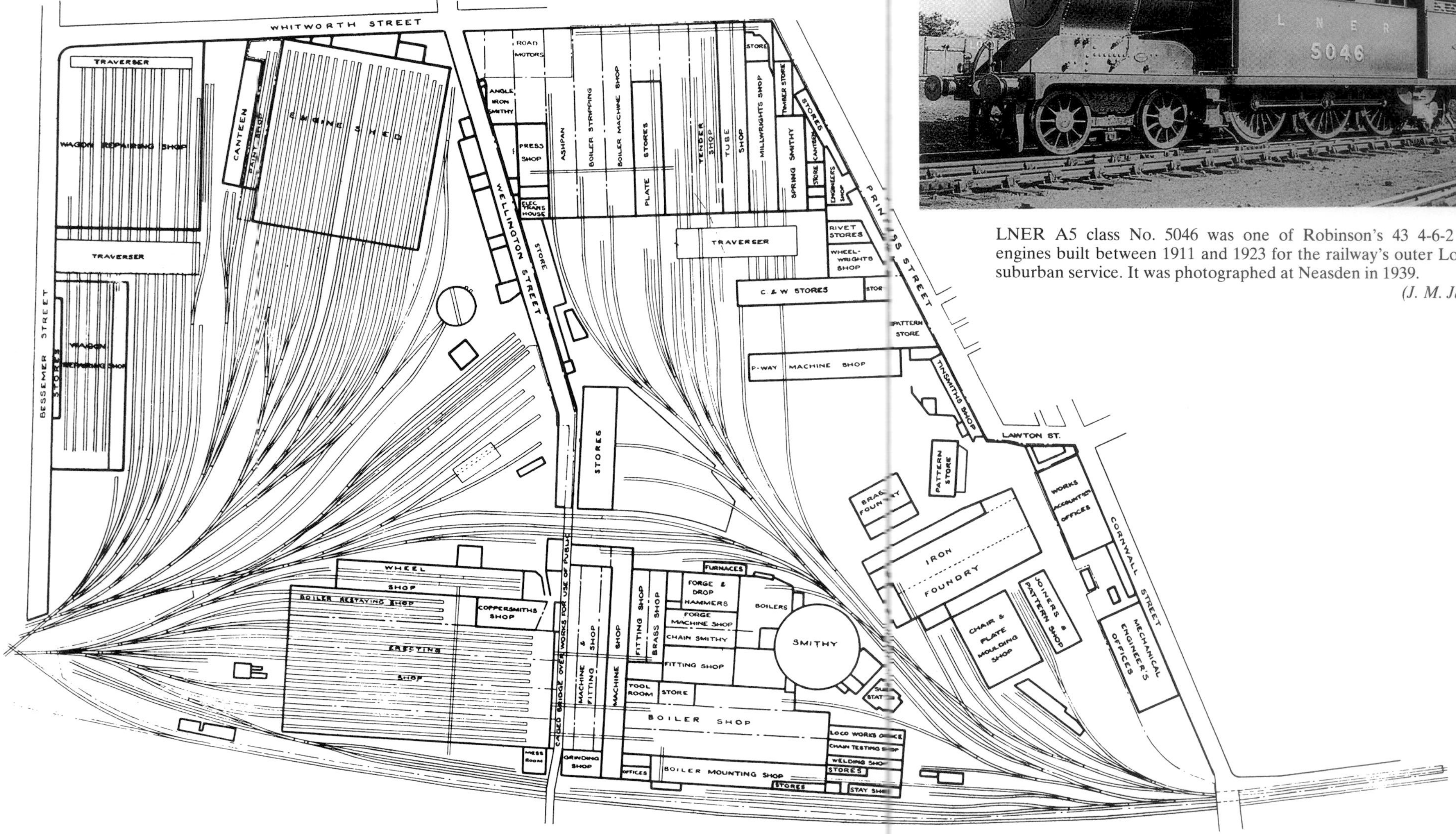

GORTON WORKS
(EASTERN REGION)

Horwich Locomotive Works

Horwich Locomotive Works was built in 1887 for the Lancashire & Yorkshire Railway Company, covering a total area of 81 acres. The first locomotive was constructed in 1889 under John Aspinall. A total of 309 2-4-2 passenger tank engines designed by Aspinall were built here between 1889 and 1910.

During the Second World War, 'Matilda', 'Cruiser' and 'Centaur' tanks were constructed at Horwich and also 20mm Oerlikon shells. An interesting point of note is that during the 1950s, Flail tanks were built for the Ministry of Supply. At its peak, over 3,000 mem-bers of staff were employed at the Works.

Horwich Works was unique in the size of its mecha-nised iron foundry. The output consisted of units for rail-chairs and brake-block manufacture and was so successful that by 1955 manufacture of these castings was left solely to Horwich. However, due to changes in modern production requirements the iron foundry has been much depleted, but remains in use today having been sold to private owners in 1987. Locomotive repairs ceased in the 1960s followed by a cessation in wagon repairs.

Horwich Locomotive Works, Lancashire.
1887 Works completed for the LYR.
1888 Locomotive construction commenced.
1889 February. First locomotive completed – 2-4-2T No. 1008.
1907 1,000th locomotive completed – excluding five locomotives built for the Works' 18in gauge tramway system.
1922 January 1st. LYR became part of the LNWR.
1923 January 1st LNWR became part of the LMSR. A total of 1,353 locomotives had been built up to this time.
1948 January 1st. Became part of BTC on Nationalisation. 1,668 locomotives built up to this time.
1952 First BR Standard locomotive built – Class 4 2-6-0 No. 76000.
1957 November. Last steam locomotive built – BR Standard Class 4 2-6-0 No. 76099, the 1,840th to be completed at Horwich.
1958 The first 0-6-0 diesel-electric shunter built – No. D3593.
1962 Last locomotive to be completed – 0-6-0 diesel-electric shunter No. D4157.
      Locomotive work ceased and carriage and wagon repairs undertaken.
1970 January. Became part of British Rail Engineering Limited.
1982 Main works closed but Foundry continued in operation.
1987 Iron Foundry sold as a going concern.
(See also Horwich Wagon Works.)

The steel foundry cast a number of wheel centres, creating the spectacular action caught in this 1919 photograph. The nearest operators seem to have had scant protection against the heat and glare!

(National Railway Museum)

75

This scene from 1913 shows the fitting shop with a group of automatic lathes.

(National Railway Museum)

The 1909 view of the boiler shop illustrates the intriguing rope-driven machinery then used for drilling stay-holes, etc. in new fireboxes.

(National Railway Museum)

Ex-Willesden Junction–Earls Court electric stock undergoing conversion at Horwich Works in 1953 for experimental use on the re-energised Lancaster–Morecambe/Heysham Line at 6,600 volts, 50 cycle ac.

(British Railways)

Erecting Shop No. 5 seen in L&Y days, had on each track at least one of Hughes' earlier 4-6-0s built in 1909-11 with Joy's valvegear. Aspinall 0-6-0 No. 889 stands on the left, before it was rebuilt with a superheated Belpaire boiler. New frame plates for a 0-6-0 are set up in the right foreground, and beyond that stands an engine with superheater and piston valves.

The machine shop in 1919 had two rows of belt-driven vertical spindle milling machines, of which the nearest one was slab milling the sweep of a built-up crank axle.

(National Railway Museum)

A 1919 scene shows the row of steam drop hammers in the smithy, which stamped steel blocks into various small components, for example, handrail pillars. Most of such items then went to another shop for machining.

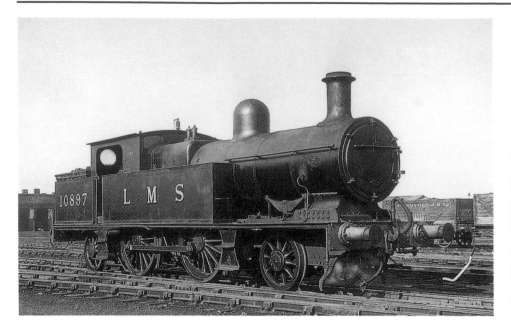

LMS No. 10897 was one of the 309 Aspinall LYR 2-4-2 passenger tank engines, built 1889-1910, which capably handled many of the L&Y and then LMS local and branch line trains in the North of England. This particular engine, when it was photographed at Rugby in 1950, was carrying an experimental self-weighing grate, aimed at accurately establishing the weight of the firebed during the course of scientific testing of locomotives.

(J. M. Jarvis)

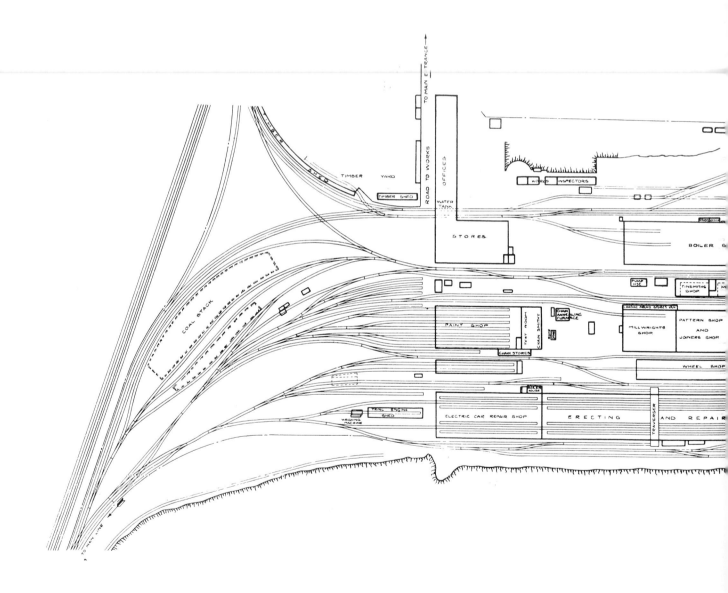

BR No. 42811, ex-LMS No. 2811, a Hughes 2-6-0 mixed traffic engine designed and built at Horwich in 1929. These engines were nicknamed 'Crabs' on account of their high and steeply inclined large cylinders. They proved to be very versatile and sturdy locomotives, hauling a wide range of trains over much of the LMS system, including a spell on the arduous Highland main line to Inverness. All of them passed into British Railways and lasted into the 1960s with three now preserved.

(J. M. Jarvis)

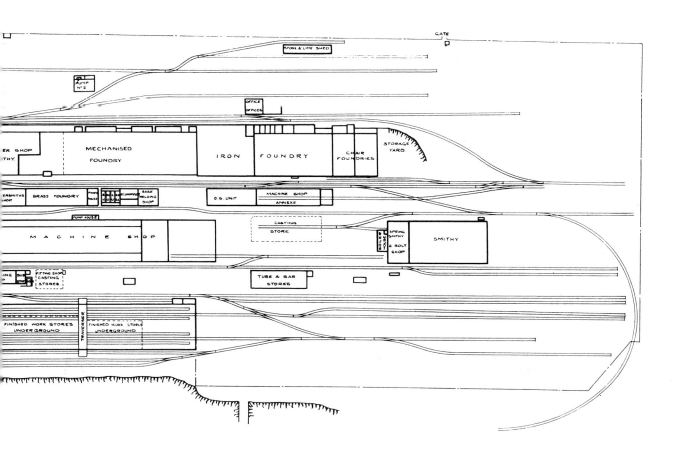

HORWICH WORKS

(LONDON MIDLAND REGION.)

Inverurie Locomotive Works

Inverurie Locomotive Works was built by the Great North of Scotland Railway Company in 1903 and covered a total site of 15 acres. It was the most northerly of all the main works, being situated some sixteen miles north west of Aberdeen. The Works constructed few locomotives, but they provided a necessary repair service.

Due to the good geographical location, the Works survived the re-organisations of 1962, but because of the decline in rail traffic, was closed in 1969.

Inverurie Locomotive Works, Scotland.
1903 Works completed for the GNSR.
1909 April. First locomotive built – Class V 4-4-0 No. 27.
1921 September. Last locomotive built – Class F 4-4-0 No. 46, the 10th locomotive to be completed at Inverurie.
1923 January 1st. GNSR became part of the LNER.
1948 January 1st. Became part of BTC on Nationalisation.
1955 Works reorganised to accommodate larger locomotives.
1962 Became part of BR Workshops Division.
1969 December 31st. Works closed.

This picture and that opposite, top, show the erection shop in June 1957 when the works were busy repairing a wide variety of engines from the Scottish constituent companies of the LNER and LMS, plus those railways' own types, as well some BR Standard locomotives.

(Brian Morrison)

Below: LNER D40 class No. 2272, photographed at Keith in 1946, was representative of the many GNSR 4-4-0 engines which operated most of the traffic, both passenger and goods. Even into British Railways days these handsome engines could be seen working or standing at most of the stations of the still-active and extensive network of lines. For hauling the more important passenger trains the LNER had transferred a number of their Great Eastern B12 class 4-6-0s, which made a fine sight in immaculate apple green livery.

(J. M. Jarvis)

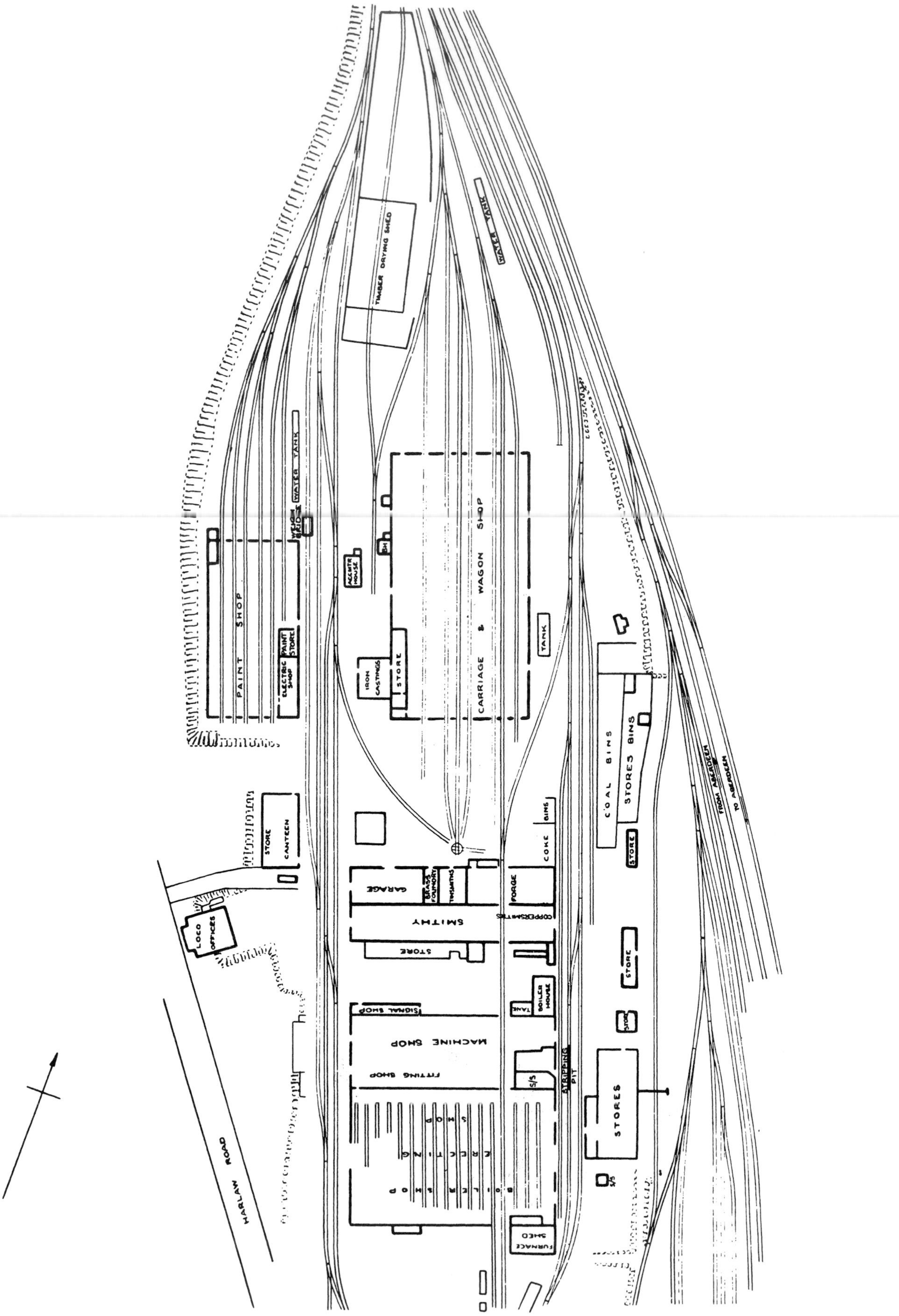

INVERURIE WORKS

(SCOTTISH REGION)

PAINT SHOP

ELECTRIC SHOP

PAINT STORE

WATER TANK

TIMBER DRYING SHED

STATE TANK

ACCOUNT HOUSE

IRON CASTINGS

STORE

CARRIAGE & WAGON SHOP

TANK

COAL BINS

STORES BINS

STORE

FROM ABERDEEN

TO ABERDEEN

STORE

CANTEEN

LOCO OFFICES

GARAGE

BRASS FOUNDRY

TINSMITHS

FORGE

SMITHY

STORE

COPPERSMITHS

COKE BINS

STORE

STORE

SIGNAL SHOP

MACHINE SHOP

FITTING SHOP

TANK

BOILER HOUSE

S/S

STRIPPING PIT

ERECTING SHOP

BOILER SHOP

STORES

S/S

FURNACE SHED

HARLAW ROAD

Kilmarnock Locomotive Works

Kilmarnock Locomotive Works was built in 1856 by the Glasgow & South Western Railway Company on a total site of 13 acres. Until 1921 the Works built new locomotives, but following the re-organisation it was involved mainly in the repair of locomotives and the breaking-up of obsolete ones.

However, by 1923 much of the heavier work had been transferred to St Rollox and a section of the Works was demolished in 1929. In 1952 the locomotive repairs finished and the Works took over the repair of the Scottish Region's cranes. It finally closed in 1959.

Kilmarnock Locomotive Works, Scotland.

1856 Works completed for the G&SWR.
1857 First locomotive built – Class 2 2-2-2.
1921 Last locomotive built, the 392th locomotive completed at Kilmarnock.
1923 January 1st. G&SWR became part of the LMSR.
1929 A section of the Works demolished, much work having been transferred to St Rollox Works.
1948 January 1st. Became part of BTC on Nationalisation.
1952 Locomotive repairs ceased.
1959 July 4th. Works closed completely.

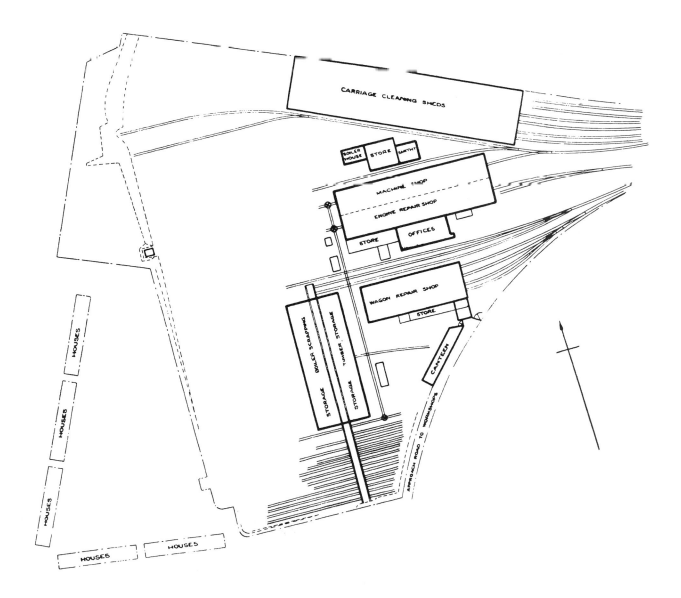

KILMARNOCK WORKS

(SCOTTISH REGION)

St Rollox Locomotive Works

St Rollox Locomotive Works was built in 1853 for the Caledonian Railway Company on a total site of 15 acres, to build and repair locomotives, carriages and wagons. Amongst its better known locomotives were the 'Cardean' 4-6-0s and 'Dunalastair' 4-4-0s.

By 1927, four years after amalgamation, new construction work ceased but St Rollox was heavily involved in repairs for LMS locomotives and carriages. By then, wagon repairs had been transferred to Barassie. By 1947, 3,382 members of staff were employed at the Works.

In 1968 Cowlairs Works were closed and all work was sent to St Rollox, to be followed by work from Inverurie and Barassie Works. Since then St Rollox Works has been renamed Glasgow Works and still carries out all repairs, including wagons, and remains as the only main works in Scotland.

St Rollox Locomotive Works/Glasgow Locomotive Works.
1853 Works constructed for the Caledonian Railway.
1854 Works formally opened and first locomotive completed – a 2-4-0.
1870 Works extended.
1884 Works extended further.
1886 4-2-2 No. 123 built.
1923 January 1st. CR became part of the LMSR.
1927 Wagon work transferred to Barassie Works and Works reorganised.
1928 Last locomotive built – 0-6-0 No. 4476.
1948 January 1st. Became part of BTC on Nationalisation.
1962 Became part of BR Workshops Division.
1968 Reorganised to become main BR works in Scotland.
1970 January. Became part of British Rail Engineering Limited.
1972 Retitled Glasgow Works.
1987 Became part of British Rail Maintenance Limited as Springburn Level 5 Depot.

The panoramic picture shows the new machine shop at St Rollox which served both locomotive and carriage activities in 1964.

(British Railways)

The electric shop situated at the end of the erecting shop in 1964, overhauled, repaired and tested the electrical equipment of diesel and electric multiple units and locomotives. Suitable cranes were installed to handle the heavier items such as traction motors and generators.

(British Railways)

The erecting shop in 1964 had three bays, formerly used for the repair of steam locomotives and seen here dealing with diesel-electric locomotives of various types including a Class 17 'Clayton' Bo-Bo diesel-electric on the left.

(British Railways)

LMS No. 14434 was photographed at Aviemore in 1947 about a year before it was withdrawn by British Railways. It was one of McIntosh's 16 handsome 'Dunalastair III' 4-4-0 passenger engines, and was rebuilt at St Rollox with a superheated boiler in 1916. When owned by the Caledonian Railway it carried a smart blue livery, decorated with lining, and must have made a fine sight.

(J. M. Jarvis)

LMS No. 16163, both built and pictured at St Rollox was one of the 23 compact 0-6-0 shunting tanks of McIntosh's design and built from 1911 to 1921. They all survived ten years or more into the British Railways era. Photographed in April 1947.

(J. M. Jarvis)

LMS No. 17316, ex-Caledonian Railway 0-6-0 built at St Rollox in 1908, seen here at Polmadie shed, Glasgow in 1947.

(J. M. Jarvis)

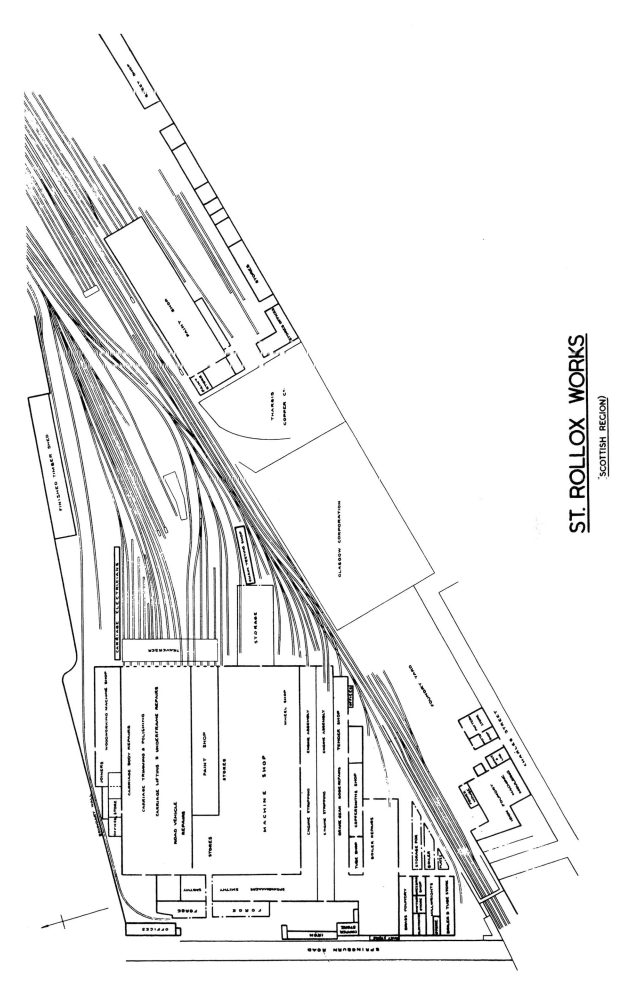

ST. ROLLOX WORKS

(SCOTTISH REGION)

Stratford Locomotive Works

Stratford Locomotive Works was built in 1847 for the Great Eastern Railway Company on a total site of 31 acres, a few miles outside of London. The first locomotives were built here in 1850, designed by J.V. Gooch. In 1909 the 2-4-2 "Crystal Palace" tank engines were built here.

By 1947, 2,032 members of staff were employed. The Works was closed in 1963 as part of the re-organisation plans, but the running shed was still used after this time for various repair and modification work.

Stratford Locomotive Works, London.

1847 Works completed for the Eastern Counties Railway.

1851 First locomotives built – six Class A 2-2-2WTs.

1862 August 7th. ECR became part of the GER.

1890 The 500th locomotive completed at Stratford.

1891 Y14 class 0-6-0 No. 930 assembled in 9¾ working hours – a new world record.

1899 The 1,000th locomotive built – Y14 class 0-6-0 No. 7510.

1923 January 1st. GER became part of the LNER.

1924 Last locomotive completed –LNER N7 class 0-6-2T No. 999E – the 1,702nd locomotive built at Stratford.

1948 January 1st. Became part of BTC on Nationalisation.

1962 Main Works closed following formation of BR Workshops Division but running shed continued in use for locomotive repair work.

Conversion from steam to diesel-electric working at the engine repair shop in 1956. Bay No. 3 shows the initial facilities for the repair of diesel shunting locomotives in foreground.

(British Railways)

Above: This picture shows the general offices, probably in the 1920s
(National Railway Museum)

LNER No. 8307, photographed on an Aylesbury bound local train arriving at Quainton Road, Buckinghamshire from Verney Junction, in 1935 when London Transport's Brill branch was still operational. These small 2-4-2 passenger tank engines were built at Stratford in 1909 and were nicknamed "Crystal Palace tanks" on account of their spacious cabs with large windows.

(J. M. Jarvis)

LNER No. 1501, photographed at Kittybrewster depot, Aberdeen in 1947, was one of the handsome B12 class ex-GER 4-6-0 express passenger engines. This engine had been built at Stratford in 1912, and was one of a number retaining smaller boilers, which the LNER transferred to work the more important trains on the former Great North of Scotland routes.

(J. M. Jarvis)

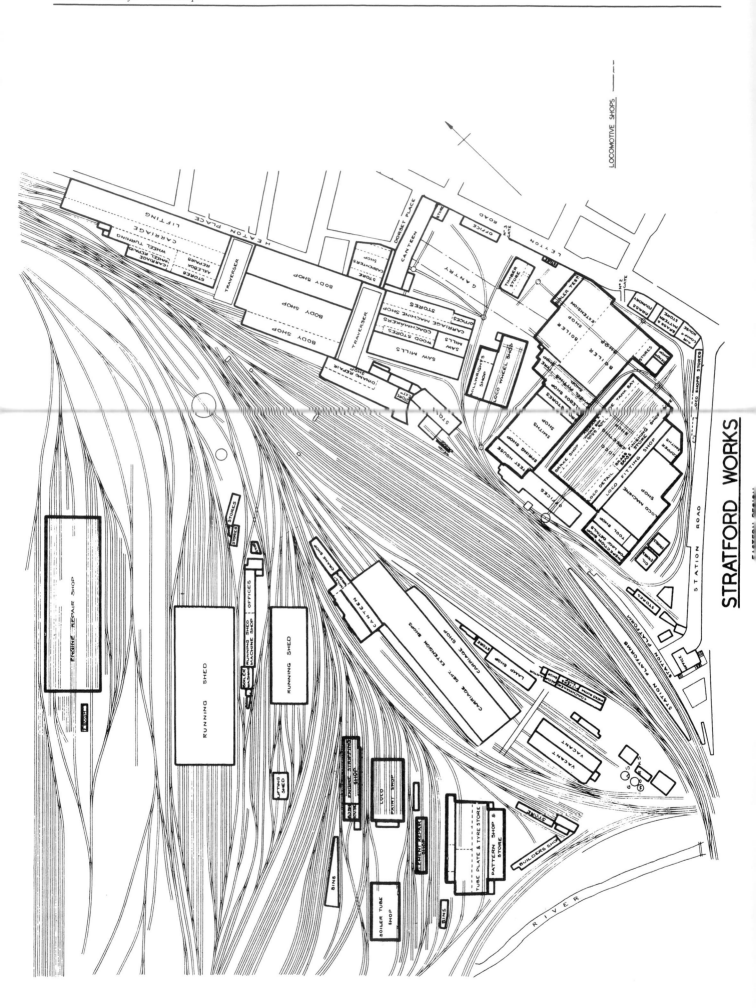

STRATFORD WORKS

Swindon Locomotive Works

Swindon Locomotive Works was built in 1842 for the Great Western Railway on a site which soon totalled 140 acres, on the recommendation of Daniel Gooch who was appointed by Brunel. It was situated on the main line from London to Bristol and South Wales. Because of the size of the site and the number of employees, a Railway Village grew up around the site, built by the Railway Company. This included a school, swimming baths, church, lending library, hospital and whole host of accompanying facilities. At one time, the number of employees in Swindon Locomotive Works was 5,758 and in the Carriage, Wagon and Stores Department, 4,157, a total of 9,915 employees.

The *Great Western* passenger locomotive was built at Swindon in 1846, being a broad gauge engine. Later, in 1903, the 4-4-0 'City' class was constructed at Swindon, to be followed by the 'Saints', 'Stars', 'Castles', 'Halls' etc as well as the unique *The Great Bear* Pacific, the first in Britain. This was later rebuilt as a 4-6-0 and named *Viscount Churchill*. A further development of the 4-6-0 was the 'King' class, the first being named after the reigning monarch at the time, *King George V*. In 1950, HRH Princess Elizabeth visited the Works and named the last locomotive of the 'Castle' class, as *Swindon* in honour of the town and her visit.

During the First World War, immense quantities of munitions were manufactured in Swindon Works, together with parts for submarines, howitzers and mines. In the Second World War, an enormous variety of items were manufactured, amongst them gun mountings, bombs, tank transmissions, dockside cranes, aircraft components, motor landing craft and complete midget submarines.

The last steam locomotive built for BR was 9F class 2-10-0 No. 92220, named *Evening Star*, at a ceremony in March 1960. Swindon also built the first diesel-hydraulic main-line locomotive for BR in 1957.

After 1962 all new building work was transferred to other works with the exception of BRUTE trolleys used for handling parcels, and only repairs were carried out at the Swindon Locomotive Works as well as the scrapping of large numbers of diesel locomotives in latter days. At this time the carriage and wagon works site was sold.

Swindon Locomotive Works were finally closed in 1986 amidst much publicity.

Swindon Locomotive Works, Wiltshire.

1842 Construction of Works and associated railway town commenced.
      November. First machinery put into operation.
1843 January 2nd. First part of Works brought into full operation.
1846 First phase of the Works completed.
      February. First locomotive completed, using some parts bought in – 'Premier' class 0-6-0 *Premier*.
      April. First locomotive built entirely at Swindon – 7ft 0¼in gauge 2-2-2 *Great Western*.
1855 May. First standard gauge locomotives built – Gooch 0-6-0s Nos 57 and 58 – despatched in wagons to the Northern Division.
1864 October. Last broad gauge locomotive built – 'Metropolitan' class 2-4-0WT *Laurel*.
1872 Standard gauge rail connection to the Works introduced.
1876 First broad/standard gauge 'convertible' locomotives built – Armstrong 0-6-0s Nos 1228–1237.
1891 August. Last 'convertible' locomotives completed as broad gauge – 2-2-2s Nos 3025–3028.
1892 May 20th/21st. Abolition of the broad gauge – last trains run.
1893 Last locomotives converted from broad to standard gauge.
1897 No. 36 built – the first 4-6-0 at Swindon – and in England.

Construction of British Railways Standard locomotive No. 75000, Class 4 4-6-0 in Swindon Works in 1951.

(British Railways)

1902 A Shop completed.

1903 No. 97 built – the first 2-8-0 at Swindon.

1908 February. No. 111 *The Great Bear* completed – the first 4-6-2 in Great Britain.

1924 April 28th. Royal visit by King George V and Queen Mary.

1948 January 1st. Became part of BTC on Nationalisation. First 0-6-0 diesel shunter built – No. 15101.

1950 Royal visit by HRH Princess Elizabeth – named 'Castle' class 4-6-0 No. 7037 *Swindon.*

1951 First BR Standard locomotive completed – Class 4 4-6-0 No. 75000.

1955 Last GWR type locomotive completed – 0-6-0PT No.1669.

1958 First main line diesel-hydraulic locomotive built – B-B Type 4 No. D800 *Sir Brian Robertson.*

1960 March. Class 9F 2-10-0 No. 92220 completed – the last steam locomotive built at Swindon and the last to be built for BR. Named *Evening Star* at special ceremony on 18th. The 5,720th standard gauge steam locomotive built at Swindon.

1962 Became part of BR Workshops Division and reorganised to include carriage and wagon works with old C&W Works being closed. New Apprentice Training School and Diesel Testing Station completed.

1964 Last main line diesel locomotive completed – Class 52 No. D1029 *Western Legionnaire.*

1970 January 1st. Became part of British Rail Engineering Limited.

1973 September. The last diesel-hydraulic locomotive to receive a classified repair returned to traffic – Class 52 No. D1023 *Western Fusilier.*

1975 Excavations in the Non-ferrous Foundry unearthed the fossilised remains of a Pliosaurus brachyspondylus.

1976 Completion of the last steam locomotive to be overhauled at Swindon by BR – preserved ex-LMS 4-6-2 No. 6229 *Duchess of Hamilton.*

1978 Refurbishment of SR emus commenced.

1980 Twenty 0-8-0 diesel-hydraulic locomotives built for metre gauge Kenya Railways.

1985 Complete closure of the Works announced. Proposed GWR 150 Exhibition cancelled.

1986-7 Works closed and site put up for sale.

1987 June. Works acquired by Tarmac Swindon Ltd for redevelopment into a community to be called Churchward. Swindon Railway Workshops Ltd established in No. 20 Shop for overhaul of steam locomotives and rolling stock.

1990 April 10th–November 4th. National Railway Museum on Tour exhibition in No. 19 Shop.

1992 June. Creation of a major new railway museum approved, to be housed in R Shop. Swindon Railway Workshops Ltd requested to vacate the premises by 30th.

Great Western Railway broad gauge locomotives waiting to be broken up or converted to standard gauge at Swindon Locomotive Works in 1892.

(Courtesy S. A. Smith)

Diesel-hydraulic locomotives under repair in Bay 5 (Erecting Shop) in 1968.

A section of No. 3 Machine Shop in 1968.

(British Railways)

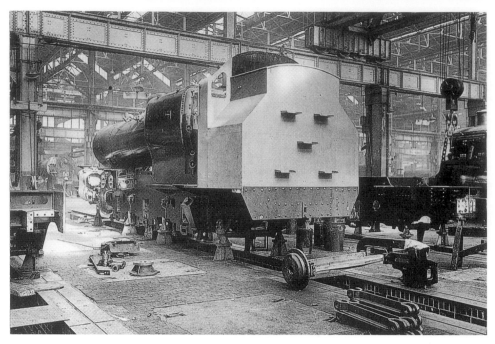

Amongst the several classes of British Railways Standard steam locomotives which Swindon shared in building were the 20 Class 3 2-6-0s and 45 corresponding 2-6-2 tank engines. Swindon drawing office had also designed these two classes. The picture shows several Class 3 2-6-2 tanks being assembled including No. 82004. It was appropriate for Swindon to be responsible for these, as the GWR had formerly built and operated a considerable number of engines of this wheel arrangement.

(British Railways)

In 1932 Collett produced the small 0-4-2 tank engines for working branch line passenger trains. Ninety-five were built, and superseded ancient 0-4-2 and 2-4-0 tank engines and other oddments. No. 4812 was photographed at Oswestry in 1946. Subsequently the 4800 series was re-numbered into 1400s. Several of the class have been preserved and can be seen in service, including No. 1466, formerly No. 4866, now at the Didcot Railway Centre.

(J. M. Jarvis)

Below: G. J. Churchward, 4-6-0 'Castle' class locomotive No. 7017, built in Swindon Locomotive Works and entering traffic in September 1948.

(British Railways)

BR Standard locomotive No. 77001, Class 3 2-6-0, all 20 of which were built at Swindon in 1954.

(British Railways)

Pictured here is *Evening Star,* Class 9F 2-10-0 No. 92220, the last steam locomotive built for British Railways, completed at Swindon in 1960

(British Railways)

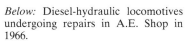

Below: Diesel-hydraulic locomotives undergoing repairs in A.E. Shop in 1966.

(British Railways)

Aerial view of Swindon Locomotive Works taken in June 1922. The General CME office is at the junction of the Bristol and Gloucester line and to its left is the original 1841 running shed. The locomotive Works Managers office is the far end of the open space at centre right. The new 'A' Shop, then only four years old, is at the top left hand corner, with the carriage building works on the extreme bottom left.

(H. R. Roberts)

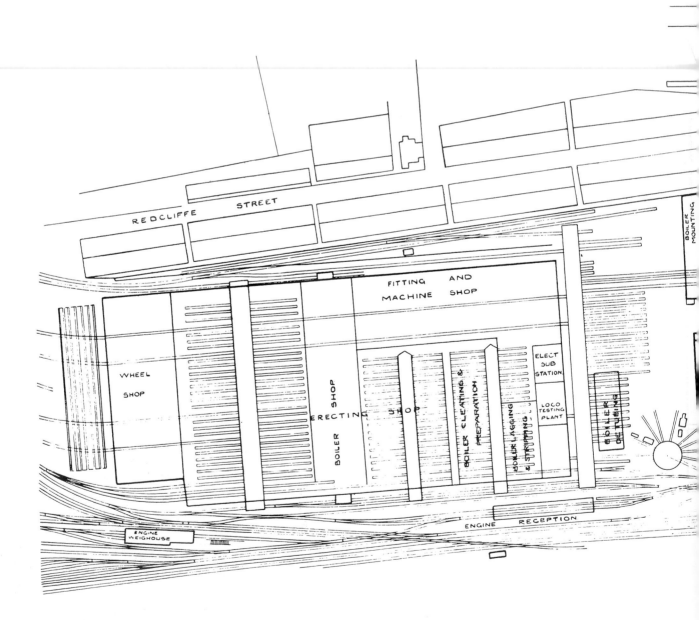

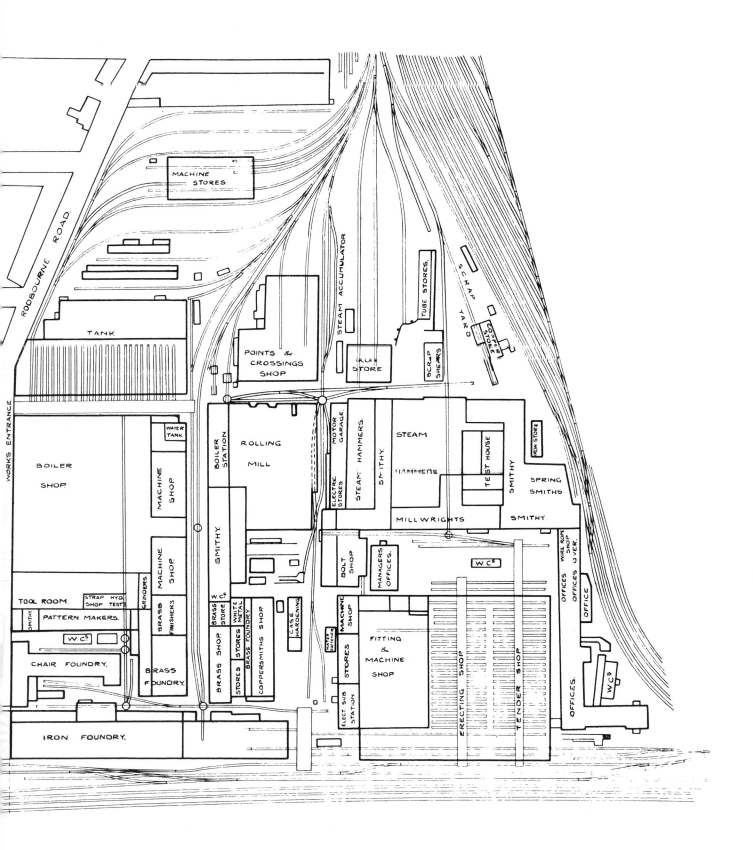

SWINDON WORKS

(WESTERN REGION)

Wolverhampton Locomotive Works

Wolverhampton Locomotive Works was built in 1855 for the Great Western Railway Company on a total site of 14 acres. The first standard gauge engine was constructed at Wolverhampton in 1859 in addition to a large amount of repair and rebuilding work on broad gauge locomotives. However, when standard gauge engines became the order of the day, Swindon Works was enlarged in preference to Wolverhampton and became the main GWR construction and repair works.

Wolverhampton continued with construction of 0-4-2 and 0-6-2 saddle tanks and some 0-4-2 and 0-6-0 side tanks until 1908 but continued with repairing and rebuilding activities.

During the Second World War, Wolverhampton Works contributed with component production in addition to locomotive repair. This repair and rebuilding work continued until 1st June 1964 when the Works was finally closed.

Wolverhampton Locomotive Works. Stafford Road, Wolverhampton.

1849 Shrewsbury & Birmingham Railway established locomotive repair shop on west side of Stafford Road.
1854 S&BR absorbed by GWR.
1855 Main works established.
1859 Former S&BR running shed converted to an erecting shop for GWR standard gauge locomotives. First locomotives built –
2-2-2s Nos 7 and 8.
1908 The last locomotives to be built at Wolverhampton – Churchward 2-6-2Ts. 794 locomotives built in total.
1935 New workshops completed to replace old buildings.
1962 Became part of BR Workshops Division.
1964 June 1st. Works closed completely.

Wolverhampton Works were opened by the GWR in 1855, and built standard gauge engines there from 1859. Tank engines were built there until 1908, including this 0-6-0 pannier tank, No. 2068 in 1899 completed as a saddle tank and modified later at Swindon. Photographed at Oswestry shed in 1946.

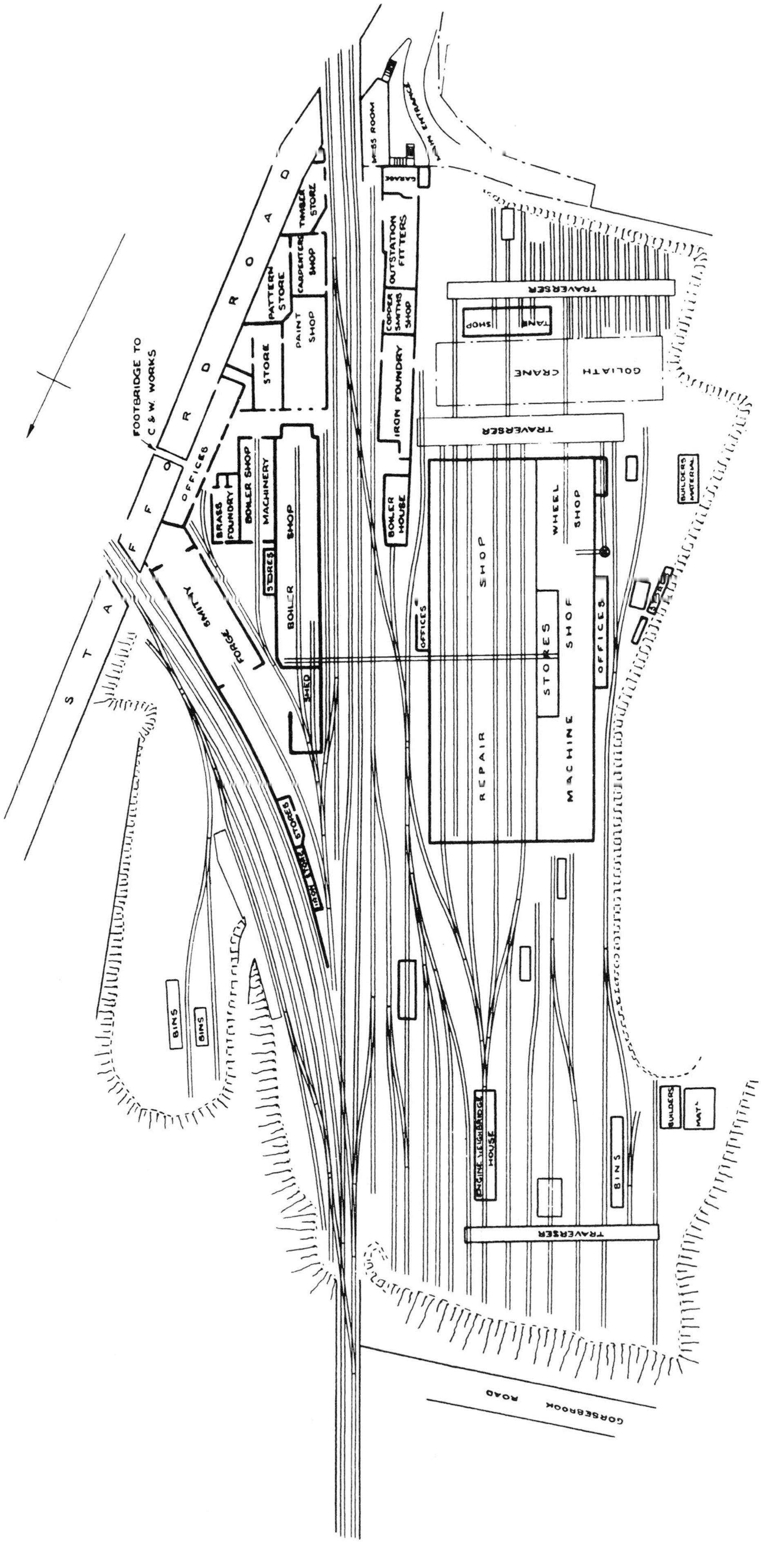

STAFFORD ROAD

FOOTBRIDGE TO C & W WORKS

OFFICES

PATTERN STORE

TIMBER STORE

CARPENTER SHOP

STORE

PAINT SHOP

BRASS FOUNDRY

BOILER SHOP

MACHINERY

STORES

BOILER SHOP

SMITHY

FORGE

SHED

USED METAL STORES

BINS

BINS

IRON FOUNDRY

BOILER HOUSE

COPPER SMITHS SHOP

OUTSTATION FITTERS

MESS ROOM

MAIN ENTRANCE

GARAGE

TRAVERSER

TRAVERSER

GOLIATH CRANE

SHOP

TANK

OFFICES

REPAIR SHOP

STORES

WHEEL SHOP

MACHINE SHOP

OFFICES

ENGINE WEIGHBRIDGE HOUSE

BINS

TRAVERSER

BUILDERS MATERIAL

BUILDERS

MATERIAL

GORSEBROOK ROAD

WOLVERHAMPTON WORKS

(WESTERN REGION)

3
Carriage Stock

Development of the Early Passenger Carriages

The first public passenger railway was opened in 1807 between Swansea and Mumbles and was powered by horses. In 1809 the first fare paying passengers with steam haulage enjoyed their world premier at a demonstration by Richard Trevithick at Euston Square, London.

On 27th September 1825 the Stockton & Darlington Railway carried the first fare paying passengers behind a steam locomotive on a public railway line. The "passenger" carriages on these first trains were very primitive and were either upgraded coal wagons with timber seats or stage coaches mounted on railway wheels.

In the early years private coach manufacturers built most of the rolling stock with scarcely any variation in design or innovation. Presumably passengers considered that the advantages of speed outweighed temporary personal discomfort. For example, when the Paddington to Bristol line opened in 1841, the timetable stated "goods train passengers will be conveyed in uncovered trucks by the goods train only, with 14 lbs of baggage allowed to each passenger". Although the journey took over nine hours, it was a vast improvement compared to 2½ days by stage coach. When the novelty of faster travel had worn off the public demanded improved standards of comfort.

Government regulations in 1844 made it a legal requirement that all railway companies had to run a minimum of one 3rd class train in each direction every day over all routes using closed carriages with seats. The train had to stop at each station, its minimum speed was defined at not less than 12 mph and the fare had not to exceed one penny per mile. These regulations were unpopular with the majority of companies who had in the past preferred to cater for the wealthier travellers, but the necessity to conform to the required standards ensured a quantum leap forward in basic design. By this time the railway companies had developed their own construction facilities and the mid 1840s saw the rectangular box body replace the multiple stage coach designs for 1st class vehicles, oil lighting was provided and the seats were padded. The 3rd class passengers were provided with a roof (originally a fare supplement was charged for this luxury!) and finally the sides of the carriages were filled in.

After the initial relatively slow development the design of rolling stock was usually compatible to the comfort and safety expectations of each generation of passengers.

Replica Liverpool & Manchester Railway First Class coach *Huskisson* alongside LMS Dining Car No. 2558.

Bodies. The demand for ever increasing production of rolling stock in the early years could not be met by the original bespoke methods of stage coach manufacture and all railway companies developed vehicle designs more compatible to flow line production. Not only did the first railway engineers have to design a passenger-carrying vehicle to travel at hitherto revolutionary high speeds, but they also had to design and manufacture the appropriate machine tools to make them. In this context their achievements were even more remarkable.

Timber was the prime material source for nearly a century. Wrought iron and then steel progressively replaced timber, originally because of its greater strength and then on a cost effective basis. Timber has now disappeared from modern stock which is of integral construction so it is perhaps of special interest to study the construction methods in the late 1920s/early 1930s, the heyday of the timber-bodied coach.

The majority of timber was imported in log form and the first conversion sawmills, with their huge bandsaws, reduced the logs into slabs for seasoning, either naturally over many years or in timber drying kilns. Each piece of timber required for coach construction was machined in fine detail, virtually to eliminate any hand fitting.

Bodysides were sub-divided into "quarters", each of which had its own special jig. The body skin was made from teak panels and the roof of T&G boards screwed to steel car lines radiused to profile with hand jack planes before being waterproofed with canvas and bedded in a white lead preparation.

Steel roofs were experimented with as far back as 1904 and a cast aluminium coach was built in the 1930s which was virtually maintenance free throughout its life.

16 gauge steel bodyside panels replaced timber prior to the Second World War and were paint "grained" to match their predecessors.

Carriage body ends being prepared in jigs ready for fitting. The teak panels having been sanded to thickness and given two coats of varnish and are being fitted in the background. Piston rod front plates, guide castings and vestibule foot plates are fixed at this stage, before assembly of the bodies.

(H. R. Roberts)

The changeover from timber to steel construction after the Second World War necessitated substantial changes in plant and machinery, although to a large extent the progressive building systems were not greatly affected. This 500-ton press was the largest capacity required to form the various pillar sections from sheet steel.

(H. R. Roberts)

A phosphate coating process was used to inhibit rust development on either the bodyside steel panels or processed sections. In the granodising plant shown here, surface grease was removed in the nearest tank, followed by a cold water wash in the second tank. The operator is lowering a stillage load of bodyside panels into the phosphating plant which is then sealed in the last tank.

(H. R. Roberts)

Left and right hand bodyside framing jigs. The heavy columns and top longitudinal slotted box section was the only permanent feature. The transverse jig plates were individually set up for each build of coach. Note the toggle clamping which gave fast assembly time necessary to load, fit and weld one complete vehicle set in an eight-hour shift. In the far background is the roof jig which, apart from producing a steel roof framework, had to skin it in the same period of time.

(H. R. Roberts)

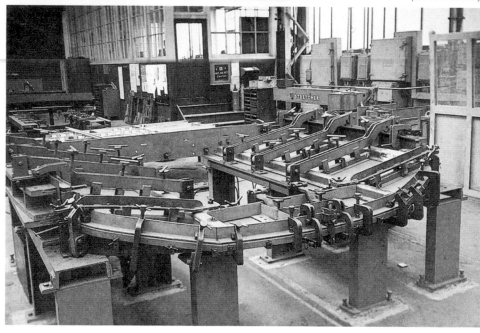

The body end jig of the same era. Note the swing-over clamping arms and the robust clamps necessary to hold the panels and body framework in close contact before welding the two together.

(H. R. Roberts)

Bogies. The demand for increased body length led to the introduction of 30ft stock in the 1850s. The Americans had by this time started to develop the principle of a long underframe, supported on two independently pivoting bogies but this idea was slow to penetrate the United Kingdom.

The GWR persevered with four separate axles under their 30ft bodies, each axle having side play in the journals to give the necessary lateral movement on curves. They did not build a bogie carriage until 1874 and this vehicle was only 46ft long so the advantages of bogie stock were obviously not fully appreciated at that stage. It would seem that the lessons were quickly learned and by 1907 70ft sleeping coaches on six-wheeled bogies were being built. It was not until sixty years later that designers matched this length again in Britain.

The construction of bogies followed the technology of that particular era. Riveted construction, utilising standard rolled steel sections, followed by hot, specially designed pressings replaced the rolled sections. One-piece cast steel bodies (Commonwealth) were all the vogue at one period until they were superseded by welded bogies, and the 1960s saw the development of B4/B5 bogies. These were probably the most efficient bogies to be used on a large scale, the dashpot suspensions eliminating the tractive stresses which had played havoc with previous designs. These bogies in turn were superseded by fabricated box section bogies which necessitated complex weld preparations giving a theoretical higher maximum speed range.

Bogie appendages have changed considerably over the years. Originally all brake actuating mechanisms were mounted on the underframe with the final on/off movement to the wheel brakes by pull rods. Modern stock usually has tread brakes mounted on the bogie itself or disc brakes on the axle. In a similar fashion the original source of power for electric lights in the coach was an axle-mounted pulley with a flat belt drive to an underframe-mounted dynamo. Secondary electric generation systems have been progressively phased out as power becomes more readily available direct from the locomotive or overhead line.

Completed motor bogie as utilised on the original 25kV ac electric multiple units.

(H. R. Roberts)

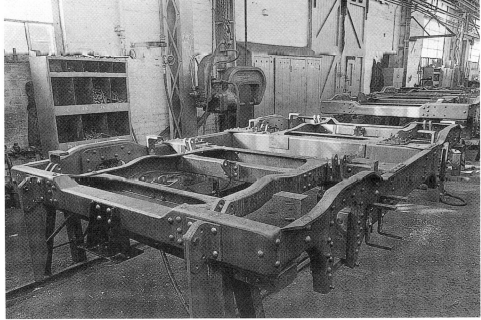

This Gresley designed bogie was re-introduced in the late 1950s to serve the first generation of 25 kV ac emus. It had knife-edge bolster suspension the life of which was extended by facing all wearing parts with Stellite.

(H. R. Roberts)

Axle-boxes and Wheel Bearings. The wheel bearings and method of lubrication have been one of the major limiting factors to engineers throughout the entire railway era. Until roller bearings were introduced after the Second World War journal bearings were the only system available. These had to be matched to very tight tolerances before burnishing with rollers. The weight of the coach was taken on brass bearings with a white metal face specially profiled to ensure a constant wedge of oil between the journal and bearing. The oil was wick-fed to the underside of the journal from a reservoir at the bottom of the axle-box.

In the early days the axle-boxes were lubricated with grease but this created even greater problems. Brunel developed large wheels in order to reduce the number of revolutions but was of minute help in minimising axle-box bearing failures.

One of the main operational hazards in the 1930s, when all companies were trying to increase average speeds and break world records, was the ever-present adverse publicity of a "hot" box. The earlier introduction of roller box bearings would have saved the white hairs on many a carriage fitter!

Brakes. Problems associated with braking steel wheels running on steel rails have been with the railways throughout their whole existence. First generation trains only had brakes on the locomotive, tender and guard's van. As train speeds increased it quickly became apparent that this system had its limitations and other coaches had to be introduced into the train set and each one fitted with a hand brake operated by additional guards. The driver signalled for brake application either on his train whistle or sometimes on a special "brake hooter". The cost of these additional guards made the engineers seek a more efficient and cost effective solution and as early as 1858 experiments were carried out with the Foy & West braking system. Unfortunately these did not prove entirely successful.

A major step forward was taken in the 1870s when the first automatic vacuum brakes were developed following Board of Trade approval in 1876. The principle of operation remained constant for nearly a century until vacuum was superseded by compressed air systems. The brakes operated on a vacuum of 22in to 25in of mercury on both sides of a piston which activated the brake. Controlled admission of air either by the

A 25 kV ac emu driving trailer built in 1961, a typical product of this era which revolutionised commuter services in particular. This being one of 76 cars of Class 309 built at York Works for the Liverpool Street – Clacton – Walton service.

(H. R. Roberts)

driver, guard or passenger emergency valve, applied by brake throughout the length of the train.

Pneumatic systems operate on a similar principle and their main advantage over the vacuum system is the higher piston pressure available which permits small diameter operating cylinders. The next improvement came in the 1960s with the fitting of disc brakes, an idea adapted from the motor car industry. Prior to this, in spite of extensive development work on brake block design the sparks generated by high speed tread braking had necessitated the fitting of spark arrestors underneath the carriage floors.

Electric stock has the advantage of being able to combine electric braking with wheel brake, and hydraulic systems will no doubt one day challenge the other methods. The "mag-lev" stock of the 21st Century will finally solve the acceleration and braking problems of steel wheels on steel rails.

Inter-Coach Drawgear. For nearly a century the link coupling with a tightening screw was the predominant form of drawgear. Early this century quad sets were built for suburban traffic, semi-permanently coupled together with male and female matching cup shaped castings.

The biggest single innovation was the introduction of buckeye couplers. These horn shaped drawgears locked together on shunting impact. They were spring loaded and could be released simply by pulling a release chain. Originally they were capable of being dropped clear of the drawgear hook which had to be available for conventional use for adjacent coaches fitted with three link couplings. The advantages of this form of drawgear soon became apparent, not the least of which being the stability displayed in accidents by the virtual elimination of jack knifing. Ultimately through various stages it developed into the solid

shank coupler now extensively used throughout the world on both freight and passenger traffic.

Carriage Heating. No heating was provided in the early days of railways and passengers brought their own foot warmers as they had done previously in the stage coach era. It was not until boiler design had improved to give a surplus supply of steam above that required for traction that the first primitive steam heating systems emerged. Steam was supplied at 60 lbs per sq inch through 2in bore pipes to heat cold trains. The pressure reduced from 10 to 20lbs according to weather after the initial warm-up period. The condensate was removed by steam traps fitted at the lowest points on the system.

Finned heaters were fitted in passenger compartments to improve heat dissipation and in principle the original concept of steam heating endured beyond the Second World War. The first generation of diesel-electric locomotives were fitted with steam boilers to supply the steam heating system.

Coaches passed through various transitional stages as electric power became available from either the locomotive or overhead electric lines until ultimately steam heating became obsolete. There were exceptions to the steam heating monopoly. Electric vehicles have always utilised their own power source and the diesel multiple units relied on Smiths heaters. Modern stock is either electrically heated or has air conditioning units fitted.

Lighting. Oil lamps were the only source of illumination for nearly sixty years until gas lighting was introduced in the 1880s.

Each carriage had its own gas reservoir(s) hung underneath the body, usually about 10 cubic feet capacity. These cylinders were charged with gas at about 10 atmospheres, to supply the burners on the coach through a reducing valve set at a pressure of approximately 1in of water.

The original gas lamps were of the fishtail or flat flame type. Incandescent mantels did not go into service until the early 1900s.

Electric lighting was first installed on one of the Royal trains in 1897 to be followed within a few years on other prestige trains. Electric lighting became standard provision for most new build carriages about the time the older stock was converted from gas fishtail jets to incandescent mantles. The quality of lighting was greatly improved in the 1950s when fluorescent tubes superseded the incandescent bulbs and voltage supplies of 240v replaced the old 24v supplies.

Passenger Environment. As a generalisation the railways have always catered for public taste in vogue at that particular period of time. The Victorians were no doubt perfectly happy with their interior French polished timber panelled compartments trimmed in crimson velvets and other bold colours. How they would have viewed our modern open clinical stock where ladies have to share toilets with gentlemen is open to conjecture!

A resume of the changes over the last thirty years will illustrate how interior design has followed public tastes during this period.

The opening top sliding window ventilation of the fifties was replaced by double glazed windows and pressure ventilation. Heating was still a separate service. In turn air conditioning units provided an all-the-year-round service.

At the end of the Second World War plastic decor gave a clean aesthetic appearance but had the disadvantage of only being available in flat sheet. The polyester resins and glass fibre provided the next generation of decor with the facility to include curvature and corners.

The next step forward was to re-design coach interiors on a 'clip-in' basis to facilitate any day-to-day renewal of damaged components. Instead of the fixed passenger seat (where the only option was whether or not the armrest was up or down) a completely new reclinable seat was designed with washable hygienic covers.

Passengers can now store their heavy luggage either in racks adjacent to the entrance doors, or between seats, instead of struggling to lift them onto the overhead luggage racks which are still available for the lighter items that in the past had to be balanced precariously on top of the heavier suitcases.

Access to the coach through either the automatically opening sliding doors or the wider platform doors is much easier than hitherto.

Progressive improvements in acoustic and thermal insulations have reduced travel noise to an absolute minimum and the guard's inter-coach communication loudspeakers are clearly discernible, The standard of illumination is probably better than most passengers enjoy at home or in their offices!

With on-board catering, telephones etc , the modern

Prototypes of new vehicle designs had to be constructed in tandem with current building programmes without distracting from production. The framing members and cant rails on the right of this picture are destined for the prototype BR Mk3 coach in July 1971, whilst in the background is one of Derby Litchurch Lane's underframe rotary jigs still constructing Mk2 stock.

(H. R. Roberts)

A prototype Mk3 coach under construction at Derby Litchurch Lane in July 1971.

(H. R. Roberts)

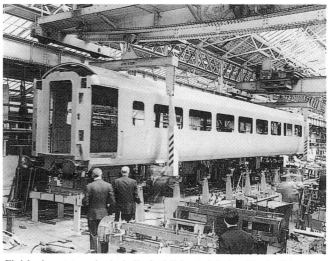

Finished prototype bodyshell of a Mk3 coach being lifted off its erection stands to be transferred down the shop for bogieing and transhipment to the Railway Technical Centre. Note the number of erection stands required to stabilise the camber until welding gave it integral strength.

(H. R. Roberts)

stock caters for public demand in a similar manner as its ancestors did.

Multiple Unit Stock. The growth in the density of passengers travelling into and out of the large cities highlighted the disadvantages of conventional train formations with a locomotive at each end. 'Push-pull' services had too many operational restraints for universal adaption. Many experimental forms were tried by the various companies, some of the early vehicles were even steam driven.

DC electric multiple unit stock with driving cabs at both ends was successfully evolved to cater for the London commuter traffic but DC supply was not commercially viable for long inter-city distances.

The LNER and GWR introduced diesel rail traction as early as 1931 but national application did not take effect until two decades later. These units tended to be underpowered as the majority relied on under-slung bus engines. Electric power was in short supply so illumination standards were only just adequate as was the blown hot air heating system. Nevertheless this stock was commercially very successful and highlighted the potential for dual cab MU stock without any restraints imposed by a DC electric supply.

In 1958 the Liverpool St., Clacton and Walton 25,000v AC stock spearheaded the new generation of multiple units. A few years later the HST was designed in dual cab MU form with the electric power supplied from on-board diesel engines as an interim design until overhead electrification was available nationwide. Their diesel-engined power system means that in the event of the failure of one engine the surviving engine can complete the journey (at a reduced speed), thus minimising any inconvenience to passengers. The success of this design could adversely effect the necessity for a conventional passenger locomotive in future years.

Special Purpose Carriages. Railways have always taken full advantage of any commercial opportunity which have arisen and have had no hesitation in building special purpose carriages to cater for public demand. For example, in the 1840s 1st class passengers had their own personal stage coaches conveyed on carriage trucks with their horses and grooms in separate horseboxes. When the journey had been completed the carriage, horses and grooms were re-united so that the owners could enjoy road travel again in their own horse and carriage. At a later stage, elegant posting vehicles could be hired for the personal use of one family or party.

A follow-on practice was to provide special trains of carriages to convey riders, horses and dogs to a hunt or the races. No matter what the social affair was, the railways could and would provide the necessary rolling stock resources. In current times the car-sleeper service is only following a tradition dating back 150 years. In a similar fashion purpose-designed vehicles were provided for:

1. Sleeping cars.
2. Dining and restaurant vehicles.
3. Newspaper distribution and sorting en route.
4. Post Office sorting and delivery vans.
5. Pigeon Vans – the railways regularly transported hundreds of pigeons to a race start point and actually released them to a timed order.
6. Invalid saloons.
7. Hospital trains in wartime.
8. Exhibition coaches.

The Mk3 at a later stage as a Royal Saloon which was built at Wolverton Works.

Carriage Works

Location	Date Built	Owning Company Pre 1923	Owning Company Post 1923	Date of Closure	Page
Caerphilly	1901	RR	GWR	1962	
Cowlairs	1843	E&GR/NBR	LNER	1968	
Derby (Litchurch Lane)	1876	MR	LMSR	–	
Doncaster	1853	GNR	LNER	1960	
Eastleigh	1891	LSWR	SR	1962*	
Gorton	1881	MSLR/GCR	LNER	1965	
Inverurie	1903	GNSR	LNER	1969	
Lancing	1888	LBSCR	SR	1962	
St Rollox	1856	CR	LMSR	–	
Stratford	1847	ECR/GER	LNER	1963	
Swindon	1869	GWR	GWR	1962†	
Walkergate	1902	NER	LNER	1962	
Wolverton	1838	LBR/LNWR	LMSR	–	
York	1884	NER	LNER	–	

* Work transferred to Eastleigh Locomotive Works.
† Work transferred to Swindon Locomotive Works.

Derby, Litchurch Lane Works with an 'Express' unit under construction for Thailand Railways.   (Colin J. Marsden)

British Railways Carriage Works

Caerphilly Carriage Works

Caerphilly Carriage and Wagon Works was built in 1901 on a 6½ acre site by the Rhymney Railway to supplement the existing locomotive works. The maximum number of carriages on site at any one time was 131. Repairs and new construction was undertaken and also a certain amount of conversion work. However from 1939, carriage repair work only was carried out, all wagon work being done elsewhere.

In May 1962 the carriage workshops were closed, with the exception of the diesel railcar work carried out in the lifting shop, with the workload being transferred to Swindon.

Cowlairs Carriage Works

Cowlairs Locomotive, Carriage and Wagon Works was built in 1843 for the Edinburgh & Glasgow Railway, later North British Railway on a site of 167 acres. It was designed and built as a combined works on the one site.

The site was closed in 1968 and work was transferred to St Rollox.

Derby Litchurch Lane Carriage Works

Derby Carriage Works at Litchurch Lane was built in 1876 for the Midland Railway on a total site of 128 acres. The Works were unique in that they were designed to handle construction from raw materials to finished stock.

In 1885 six-wheeled carriages were being produced requiring 26 coats of primer, filling, paint and varnish. The entire process required three weeks. Modern coaches require only four coats and take only five days to complete. By 1948 the Litchurch Lane site was the principal carriage and wagon works of the LMR, producing all-steel carriages, and the Works completed 261 carriages during 1949, when a total of 5,127 staff were employed. During later years, all-aluminium vehicles were built.

During the Second World War aeroplane wings were manufactured at the Works. In 1962 new wagon work ceased and repairs were drastically cut and the Works were reorganised and adapted to cater solely for carriage work which continues to this day.

A Midland Railway lavatory composite brake coach built at Derby Carriage Works in 1890. This clerestory-roofed vehicle was designed by David Bain.

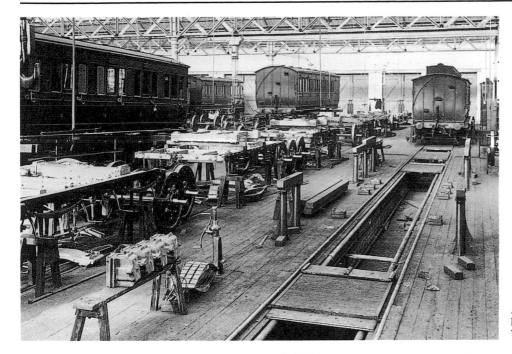

An early photograph of the carriage lifting shop in Derby Litchurch Lane Works.

Derby Carriage and Wagon Works sawmill for the manufacture of timber components, 1922.

Steam hammer in 'J' shop in 1939-1945 (note the female operator).

Log sawing showing a 2ft 6in diameter log being sawn into planks in the sawmill in 1939. Since those days railway carriage bodies have been made of steel or aluminium.

The annealing plant in 'J' shop in 1949.

(British Railways)

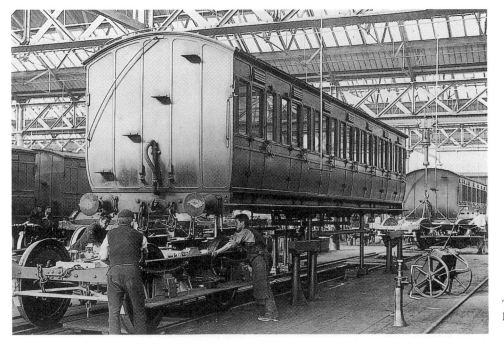

The carriage lifting shop at Derby Litchurch Lane Works in the 1880s.

(National Railway Museum)

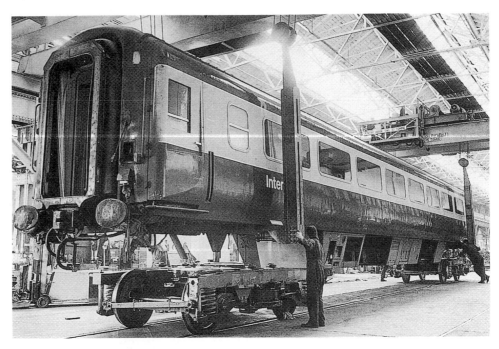

Lifting modern carriages nearly one hundred years later at Derby Litchurch Lane Works, 1981.
(British Railways)

Timber body on a steel underframe, a transitional stage from the all-timber coach to the all steel vehicle. The 'quarters' ie the body framing between doorways, were prefabricated on jigs before assembly on the underframe. The two men on the left are cramping one down before securing to the bottomside with steel angle brackets.

(National Railway Museum)

Elegant interior of a Bain first class dining car built in 1906. Judging by the amount of cutlery on the table the menu would appear to be compatible with the opulant surroundings.

A general view of the Polyester Shop in 1969.

(British Railways)

Assembly of main underframe in jig for Mk 3 coaches, Derby Litchurch Lane in 1971.

(British Railways)

British Rail's Advanced Passenger Train, built at Derby entered revenue earning service for a brief period in December 1981.

(BREL)

London Transport Executive stock manufactured at Derby Litchurch Lane in 1962.

(BREL)

Left: One of several standard gauge electric locomotives employed at Litchurch Lane Works specifically for hauling carriage traversers.

(Mike Tye)

Below: A proud milestone in the works history, No. W50836 the 500th diesel rail car to be built at Derby Litchurch Lane. Although these vehicles were only basically a rail coach powered by underframe-suspended bus engines, they performed sterling service on commuter lines throughout the UK over many decades.

(British Railways)

Derby Litchurch Lane Works has also built coaches for export. This particular vehicle was destined for Guinea Bauxite Mines, Kamsa, to be hauled at the end of wagon ore trains between the mine and the port. The works adapted the BR Mk2 design, which was in production at that time, to match the client's specification for buffing and drawgear, brakes, trimming and more powerful air-conditioning.

Diesel railbus R3, (No. RDB977020) built jointly by British Rail Engineering Limited and British Leyland at Litchurch Lane Works, Derby in 1982.

(BREL)

Doncaster Carriage Works

Doncaster Carriage Works was built in 1853 for the Great Northern Railway Company on a 61 acre site as a carriage repair site but was later re-organised to cater for construction and repair of carriages. The first coach was built here in 1866 and the first dining car in the UK was built here in 1879. All type of carriage construction was undertaken at Doncaster from kitchen cars to main-line corridor vehicles. Two trains were built at Doncaster for the "Flying Scotsman" service in 1924 including a triple restaurant car using electric cooking.

The building shop was burnt down in December 1940 and not fully replaced until 1949 but as a far more modern construction. At this time, 1,585 members of staff were employed at the Carriage Works.

In 1960 all carriage construction was discontinued at Doncaster, but repair work has been continued, including wagon repairs from 1965, remaining part of BREL from 1970 to 1987. It was then sold to the private sector to become the basis of the subsequently very successful RFS Industries.

King Edward VII royal day saloon No. 395 built at Doncaster in 1908. All the major railway companies had their own royal trains, and competition between them was very keen.

(National Railway Museum)

Third class dining car built in 1900 at Doncaster for the Great Northern Railway, with a high standard of elegance for its class.

The old method of plate edge preparation prior to welding – hand feed only.

(British Railways)

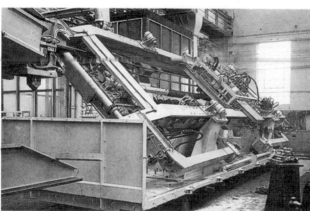

Left: The Freightliner grapple frame built at Doncaster Works in 1968 for lifting containers at Freightliner depots.

Below: View down the diesel multiple unit repair shop taken in 1970, which illustrates the mixed nature of the workload. The bodies have been re-mounted on to wheeled trestles by means of the overhead cranes, one of which can be seen in the background. Note the wall-mounted jib crane in the left foreground, a common practice under overhead cranes in all works, and the portable air winch in the right foreground.

(British Railways)

Eastleigh Carriage Works

Eastleigh Carriage and Wagon Works was built in 1891 for the London & South Western Railway Company on a 54 acre site. Work was transferred to the site from Nine Elms in London and William Panter became the first Superintendent of the Works. The Works built new carriages and containers and repaired carriages, wagons and containers. New carriage building ceased at the outbreak of war in 1939 and work then concentrated on conversion of vehicles into ambulance trains and building motor boats, landing-craft, pontoons, rocket-guns and Horsa glider tail units. In 1945 carriage construction was resumed with all-steel suburban electric coaches.

Carriage work was transferred to the Locomotive Works when the carriage site closed in 1962. However, prior to this six locomotives were constructed in the Carriage Works – the first batch of electro-diesels, completed in 1962.

From 1970 emu and dmu stock was overhauled for the Southern Region as well as some for the Eastern Region. (See also Eastleigh Locomotive Works)

The Trimming Shop layout referred to in the following photograph. Note the overhead moving conveyor belt which transported both incoming and re-trimmed items.

The carriage repair layout at Eastleigh was probably the most highly organised in BREL despite its complex workload. Vehicles passed down one side of the shop for stripping, before returning on the other side for re-assembly. Items such as trimming had to cross over the width of the shop before they were re-assembled on the vehicle.

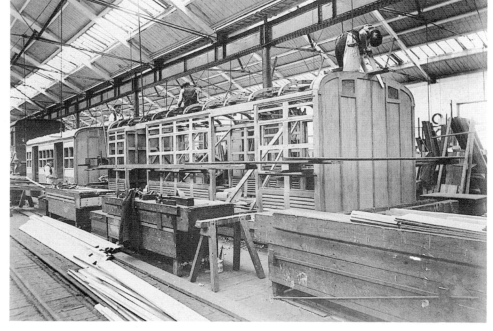

There are several interesting features in this old photograph. The flimsy scaffolding, with the tool boxes on it to trip up any unobservant colleagues would give the modern safety officer apoplexy, especially after he had seen the naked electric light bulbs dangling from the gas pipes! The vehicles, has louvred sides and no windows,

(National Railway Museum)

Gorton Carriage Works

Gorton Carriage and Wagon Works was built in 1881 by the MSLR on a six acre site near to the Locomotive Works. Only light repairs to carriages were undertaken as the facilities were not large enough for heavy repair work. The Works were closed in 1965.

Inverurie Carriage Works

Inverurie Works was built in 1903 for the Great North of Scotland Railway on a 15 acre site. The site combined locomotive, carriage and wagon works. During 1947 a total of 240 staff were employed on heavy and light carriage repair work and wagon work. The Works were closed on 31st December 1969.

Lancing Carriage Works

Lancing Carriage and Wagon Works were built in 1888 for the London, Brighton & South Coast Railway on a 42 acre site. At this time wooden carriages were constructed and all wagon work was transferred to Lancing from Brighton Works. Experimental work on a double decker carriage was carried out here, but later abandoned.

During the Second World War, Horsa glider tail units were built here. General Montgomery stated he had information that the Germans planned to land on the nearby beaches and use the factory at Lancing Carriage Works for maintaining their vehicles. From then until the end of the war, either the Works Manager or his assistant slept at the Works to enable vital parts of machinery and their documentation to be removed at short notice and taken inland by a train which was kept ready for such use.

In 1954 proposals were put forward for the undertaking of repairs to coaches for the Southern Region, plus some electric multiple-unit stock. These were never implemented as the Works were closed in 1962.

St Rollox Carriage Works

St Rollox Carriage and Wagon Works were built in 1856, along with the Locomotive Works. They were rebuilt in 1882 when the Works were extended and reorganised. By 1923 it was the major works of the LMS Northern Division but no more new construction was undertaken. In 1929 wagon repair work was transferred to Barassie and St Rollox concentrated on repairs to its some 5,000 carriages.

In 1962 the Carriage Works were amalgamated with the Locomotive Works and became known as Glasgow Works from 1972. In 1964 the whole of the Carriage Works side was gutted and modernised and a 7-ton internal traverser was installed to replace overhead cranes.

Ex-LBSCR, Lancing-built 3rd class brake coach, BR No. S4154 at Cowes, Isle of Wight in July 1964.

(Peter Nicholson)

Stratford Carriage Works

Stratford Carriage Works was built in 1847 for the Eastern Counties Railway Company on 27 acres. All smithing work was done by the Locomotive Works nearby. A variety of heavy and light repairs were undertaken. The Works closed in 1963 with a staff of 1,498, the repair work being transferred to Doncaster.

Right: An experiment in the 1930s to introduce the concept of a moving belt repair system to carriage lifting. Vehicles were hauled down the shop at Stratford by means of a dragline powered by the machinery in the foreground of the picture. Specified stages ensured that repair facilities and material could be concentrated where required. The system was later abandoned when it was realised that the belt could only move at the speed of the heaviest repair which trapped lighter repairs in the belt.
(National Railway Museum)

Below: Timber coach construction of an earlier era at Stratford. Note the teak bodyside panelling which was a feature of stock of this period. The roof timber trusses give some idea of the age of the building.
(National Railway Museum)

Swindon Carriage Works

Swindon Carriage and Wagon Works was built in 1869 for the Great Western Railway Company on a 137 acre site. The early carriages were broad gauge but many were later converted to 'narrow' gauge. In 1870 3rd class carriages had bare board seats, but from 1878 all seats were upholstered, and by 1882 lavatories were installed in the 1st class compartments. Before 1900 sleeping cars and 1st class restaurant cars were constructed at Swindon.

The Works were separated from the Locomotive Works by the Paddington to Gloucester line. The Carriage and Wagon Works were divided into construction and repair sites by the Paddington to Bristol line.

By 1950 the Carriage and Wagon Works employed 4,300 men. During the 1950s, all-steel bodied integral coaches, diesel multiple train sets and 1st class restaurant cars were constructed at the Works. They also boasted a disinfecting unit for passenger vehicles and wagons. The Works finally closed in 1962, with work transferred to the Locomotive Works which was appropriately re-organised.

Right: Victorian elegance of the coaches in service with the GWR's New Milford Boat Trains in 1900 which reduced the scheduled nine hour journey down to 6½ hours. Of standard clerestory design, all vehicles were fitted with electrical wiring, inside chain communication and an attendant's electrical bell system.

A BR Mk1 Restaurant Car built at Swindon in 1957. The Mk1 design first entered service in 1950 as the 'Festival of Britain' train and was ultimately superseded by the Mk 2 design in late 1963, the prototype of which had also been built at Swindon earlier that year, although many coaches remained in traffic for a considerable time thereafter.

(Swindon Railway Museum)

A 'Dreadnought' restaurant car of c1905, No. 9529, a design 10ft longer and 1ft wider than previous builds which, coupled with a full body instead of a clerestory, revolutionised interior spaciousness. A Churchward design which kept abreast of American practices. Many of the small toplights above the windows were blanked off as years went by.

(Swindon Railway Museum,

A Hawksworth corridor 3rd coach No. 855, one of the last GWR coaches to be built at Swindon and a fitting tribute to the last of the Great Western CME's, F. W. Hawksworth, a Swindonian by birth who started as an apprentice in 1898 and became Chief Mechanical Engineer in 1941.

(Swindon Railway Museum)

Walkergate Carriage Works

Walkergate Carriage and Wagon Works was built in 1902 for the North Eastern Railway Company on a 14 acre site next to Walkergate station, to carry out repair work. The main building was destroyed by fire in August 1918 and much of the stock contained was destroyed.

The Works employed 508 people in 1949. In 1962 the Works were closed and wagon repair work went to Shildon and York.

Wolverton Carriage Works

Wolverton Carriage and Wagon Works was built in 1838 for the London & Birmingham Railway Company on an 89 acre site. It was built as a locomotive repair centre but the locomotive work ceased in 1877 and attention turned to carriage construction and repair. By 1924, 4,500 members of staff were employed.

During the Second World War, Horsa glider sections, 8,442 assault boats, bridge pontoons, motor dinghies, steam launch boilers and Balsa rafts were constructed and the conversion of nearly 700 vans into armoured vehicles was undertaken at the Works.

In 1962 general construction work ceased except for saloons for the Royal train. HRH Queen Elizabeth II visited to inspect the Royal train on more than one occasion.

Since 1977, some other new work has been undertaken, including vehicles for the Post Office, sleeping cars etc.

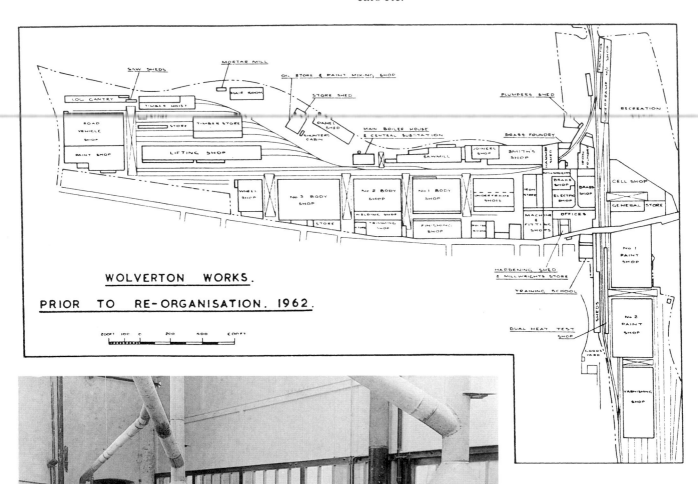

WOLVERTON WORKS.

PRIOR TO RE-ORGANISATION. 1962.

For over half a century, the manufacture of electric cells for all rolling stock was centralised at Wolverton. This photograph was taken in 1930 and shows the plate manufacturing section.

(National Railway Museum)

Generally speaking, until the Second World War, the only jobs open to women were either as typists or seamstresses in the trimming shop. Many railways actually preserved the latter jobs for widows of their own staff. This photograph shows the women in action in 1933, segregated from the men.

(National Railway Museum)

Six-wheel bogie built for the royal train which is still kept at Wolverton when not in use. It was one of the routine duties of the works manager to accompany the royal train when it went out on service.

(National Railway Museum)

Underframe for the Queen's saloon.
(National Railway Museum)

Carriage underframe shop in 1933, with the underframe road on the left and the bogies on the right. The triangular shaped wooden floor blocks are made from the teak inserts of Mansell wheels which had been scrapped in the previous century.

(National Railway Museum)

BR Carriage Department Wolverton No.7 LNWR "Special Tank" 0-6-0ST, one of the works shunters, seen at Rugby in February 1949.

(J.M. Jarvis)

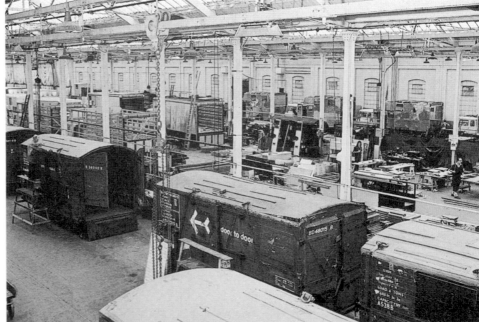

Container repairs and road vehicle construction in the Road Vehicle Shop in 1971. The shop was laid out to build and repair the bodyworks of road vehicles to MoT standards, using metal, wood and reinforced plastics. Other activities included container repairs and work for other railway departments, eg level crossing gates.

The Lifting Shop: bogie washing machine and bogie frame lift in 1971.

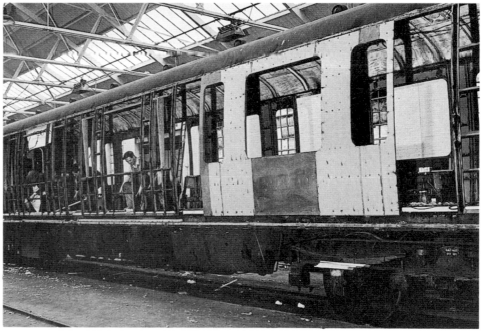

A vehicle undergoing body conversion in the carriage 'Heavy' Repair Shop in 1971.

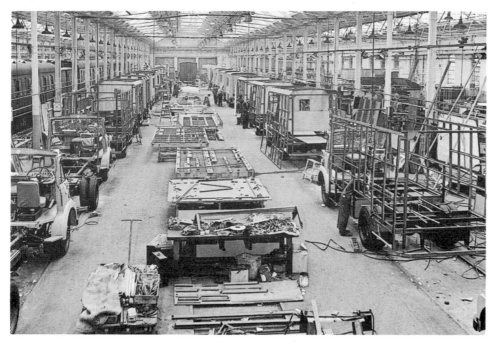

Personnel Carrier progressive layout in the south bay of the West Repair Shop, set out with guillotines and presses for the production of body panels and pressings, phosphating plant for corrosion resistance, welding and bench areas for the production and repair of components.

The Trimming Shop carries out all upholstery repairs as well as complete retrimming. A special feature of this shop is the sewing machine section operated by female labour for the manufacture of curtains and soft furnishings. This shop also undertakes the laying of linoleum and cleaning of carpets etc. This photograph shows trimming of omnibus seats, a private party contract.

The Plastics Shop manufacturing large and small components, mostly with polyester resin and usually reinforced with glass fibre for strength. This process was originated, as far as railway workshops were concerned, by Wolverton in 1953. The photograph shows the manufacture of glass reinforced plastic components.

York Carriage Works

York Carriage Works was built in 1884 for the North Eastern Railway Company on a 45 acre site, nearly twenty years after the Wagon Works. By 1982, 2,600 staff were employed at the Works.

Since 1958, multiple unit electric stock has been built here. Now the Works is one of only two Works manufacturing new carriage stock for British Rail and as such is one of the busiest railway workshops in operation today. From 1st January 1970 it became part of BREL and is now part of BREL (1988) Ltd.

The complexity of the wiring on the early 25,000 volt multiple units can be judged from this underframe layout, prior to installing the equipment cases which tend to conceal the intricacy of work underneath.

(British Railways)

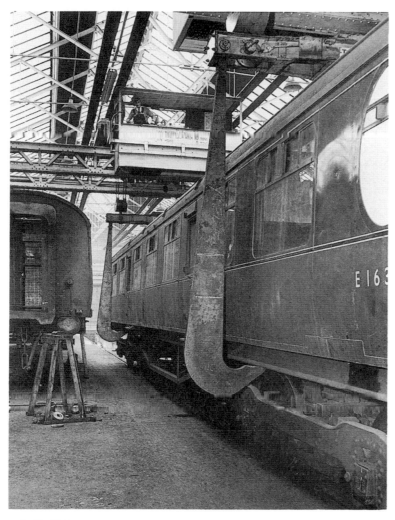

The general practice in all works for lifting coaches on and off their bogies by means of two cranes. Note the irregular depth of the panel patching at the base of the bodyside. Shortly after this photograph was taken the depth of these repairs was standardised so that new panels could be manufactured in bulk, instead of bespoke sizing as had occurred on this vehicle.

(British Railways)

Staff at work in a BR Mark 1 standard kitchen car, built at York in 1951.

A later product from York Works, a Class 312 electric multiple unit (built 1975-78) en route to King's Cross.

(British Railways)

Class 507 electric multiple unit stock built at York for Merseyrail in 1979.

(British Railways)

Until such time as all wagons were fitted with train brakes, some of the locomotives hauling freight trains had problems in braking within specified limits. As a temporary expedient diesel brake tenders were built at York from condemned carriages. The underframes were cut down and re-welded to minimum bogie rotation clearances. All brakegear was re-positioned on top of the underframe and the remaining space filled with cast iron weights. The original steel roof sweeps were utilised with everything except the steel sheeting being recovered materials.

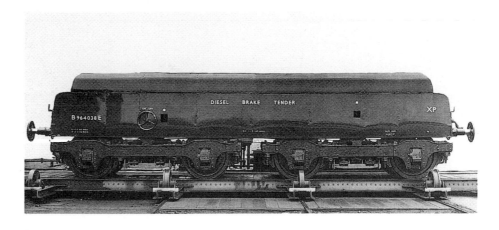

Class 313 electric multiple unit stock under construction in York Works in 1976.

(British Railways)

Pre-production Class 165 coach, No. 00000, built as a 'real' vehicle, used for production training and equipment positions, April 1991. Subsequently sent for scrap.

(Colin J. Marsden)

4
Freight Stock

The development of Industry and the growth of railways are synonymous.

The early railway developers were not only brilliant innovative engineers, but were also quick to recognise future business developments and built the appropriate stock to monopolise the business.

This policy of benevolent despotism in assessing and seizing market opportunities carried on for over a century until challenged by the growth in road transport. Unfortunately this occurred when the railways were under bureaucratic financial control and one is entitled to wonder whether I.K. Brunel and Robert Stephenson would have surrendered to the political edits over the last four decades. They certainly overcame similar challenges many times during their periods in office.

Early Developments. Coal was transported in horse drawn wagons as early as 1700. The manufacturer of an 'L' shaped cast iron rail in 1780 used in conjunction with cast iron wheels dramatically reduced friction losses and revolutionised pay loads.

This system was ultimately superseded by a flanged wheel running on a flat rail, a principle which is still used today.

Freight railways were born when a steam locomotive hauled a 10 ton wagon load in Wales in 1804. The first steam locomotives were developed to haul wagons, and passenger traffic was an afterthought.

Development of Freight Rolling Stock. In the 1840s flat wagons were built to carry passengers' own road carriages, whilst their horses and grooms were conveyed in the first primitive horse boxes – if you were attending a fox hunt there were special wagons to transport the pack of hounds!

Purpose-built parcel vans, open and covered goods vans were quickly built to cater for the ever-increasing and varied demands for these services.

The transportation of fish and milk without the inconvenience of refrigeration facilities were assisted by incorporating slatted body sides and end ventilators to generate an air flow around the churns. As a general rule, such vehicles were fitted to run on the faster passenger trains if required.

By 1850 the rail network covered main routes to most parts of the country and London was linked to Edinburgh and Glasgow – relatively long distances for the primitive buffing, drawgear, spoked wheels and grease axleboxes of that era.

The latter half of the 19th Century saw major developments in wagon design and manufacture. Vacuum brakes, improved journal and axlebox designs and six-wheel capability permitted overall size and carrying capacity increments.

Apart from the canal and barge network (which railways were buying up in order to close down the canal traffic) virtually all inter-city freight was carried by rail.

The design of railway wagons evolved from the chaldron wagon pulled by horses along a track of wood in the North East of England. All parts used in the construction of this wagon were processed by hand; trees from the local district were sawn, and cut to the required shape to form the frame-members. The design of frame was generally two sole-bars, the ends of which acted as buffers; two head-stocks tenoned into the sole-bars; and two diagonals which were fitted full length of the frame and tenoned into the head-stocks; they were half-jointed at the point of intersection to each other.

All tenon-joints were pegged; hand-made spikes, and nails with iron bands, securely held the parts together. Cast-iron tyres were fitted to wooden cart-wheels, rotating on an axle fitted with the ordinary cart bearing. Springs were unknown and hand-forged chains were used for couplings, whilst wooden brake-blocks operated by a single lever were used to provide braking power.

These wagons had a capacity of between 1 and 3 tons. There was no standard type of construction as each small colliery or works built the wagons to its own design. By 1860 a wooden-buffer railway wagon had been evolved which met the transport needs of the small industries of that period.

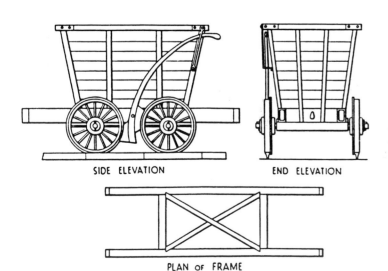

SIDE ELEVATION   END ELEVATION

PLAN OF FRAME

Fig. 2. Early chaldron wagon.

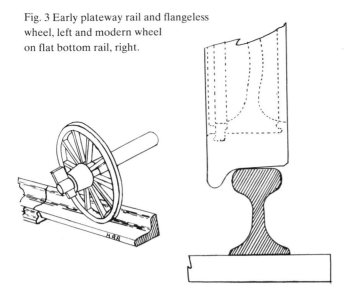

Fig. 3 Early plateway rail and flangeless wheel, left and modern wheel on flat bottom rail, right.

About 1880 the railway companies and private owners of wagons agreed to set up a joint committee to consider and examine the design of a railway wagon which incorporated the principle of the spring-buffer, and several improvements in structural strengths of wagon parts. This committee was named The Railway Clearing House and it was decided that all questions relating to constructional details of privately-owned wagons must be submitted to this body, and that the decision given must be conformed to by all parties.

Improved suspensions in the early 1900s resulted in some six-wheel designs reverting to four wheels without any reduction in load carrying capacity. Boyce

wagons appeared in greater numbers and apart from conventional loads of steel were used to carry such varied loads as army tanks and arms equipment. The army's elephants incidentally, were carried in covered carriage trucks.

Various experiments were tried to develop a combined road/rail vehicle but these were not found to be cost effective, although recent developments in this area appear to be finding some success.

Attention then switched to container traffic, originally of timber construction, and finally to steel. The important factor in the latter's success was the establishment of specialised handling facilities in the container depots.

The higher speeds and heavier train loads which coincided with diesalisation left unfitted freight trains with inadequate braking capacity and for a while Diesel Brake Tenders were provided. These were phased out following conversion of the wagons to power braking.

Road competition started to have a serious impact in the 1950s and this, coupled with a policy decision to abandon all freight traffic except that which was very profitable, resulted in a large portion of the fleet being scrapped.

The smaller scope of activities made it possible to design wagons for specific activities such as merry-go-rounds where they are literally part of a continuously mechanised moving chain.

In a similar manner to their sister coaching stock the requirements for routine maintenance have been drastically reduced following design refinements. Modern freight stock is relatively expensive to build but has a high utilisation and life expectancy.

Unlike the world famous locomotive works Crewe Carriage and Wagon Works was never regarded as a Main Works. It was primarily a carriage repair works but new ballast wagons are present in this 1965 view.

Cattle wagons nearing completion in the 1920s at Newton Heath Works.

(National Railway Museum)

Design Improvements To Freight Vehicles

Wheel Bearing Lubrication. Lubrication of wheel bearings was a problem from 1825 as the rather basic machinery finishes available coupled with grease lubrication was not an ideal combination.

The development of an oil feed to replace grease improved matters as did finish burnishing of the journal until the introduction of roller boxes finally solved the problem.

The potentially high cost of converting existing wagons from journal to roller boxes was mitigated by machining down the original wheel sets and using slave adaptors to hold a basic roller box.

This improvement in turn led to the opportunity of using smaller diameter wheelsets which lowered the deck height of wagons to carry higher loads.

Wheel Sets. Wrought iron spoked wheel sets were much favoured until superseded by solid steel disc wheels. These were then adapted to take a renewable steel tyre which could be changed without destroying the mating face.

The final stage, detailed in the preceding paragraph, where smaller diameter wheels have been adopted has seen this policy of exchangeable tyres reverting back to solid wheels again as modern oil injection facilities permit wheels to be replaced without scoring the axle seat.

Braking. Braking by locomotives on unfitted trains resulted in a sequential shunting impact throughout the train set which did not do the wagons or their contents much good.

This situation was progressively improved as wagons were converted to vacuum braking but it was a relatively slow programme.

In recent years all new wagons have been built with air brakes which allow higher running speeds and smoother braking.

Wheel Suspension. The friction suspensions fitted between leaf springs and the wagons since the 1970s have improved riding characteristics tremendously which in turn has reduced wear and tear on other component parts.

Structural Design Improvements. The bottleneck which occurred when loading wagons through a centre set of doors has been eliminated by designing wagons with full length doors yet still retaining adequate body strength to meet the exigencies of high speed rail movement.

Automatic Train Unloading. On a similar principle to the air-brake system it is now possible to open automatically all doors on a hopper wagon train thus eliminating the previous slower individual manual operation.

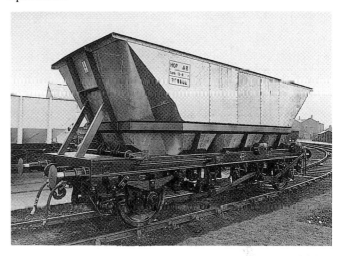

A high-capacity hopper wagon as built in large quantities at Shildon Wagon Works.

Wagon Works

| Location | Date Built | Owning Company | | Date of Closure |
		Pre 1923	Post 1923	
Ashford	1850	SECR	SR	1982
Barassie	1901	GSWR	LMSR	1972
Bromsgrove	1840	MR	LMSR	1964
Cowlairs	1842	NBR	LNER	1968
Derby (Litchurch Lane)	1876	MR	LMSR	–
Doncaster	1889	GNR	LNER	1965*
Earlestown	1853	LNWR	LMSR	1963
Eastleigh	1891	LSWR	SR	1968
Faverdale	1923	NER	LNER	1962
Gorton	1881	MSLR/GCR	LNER	1963
Horwich	1887	LYR	LMSR	1982
Inverurie	1903	GNSR	LNER	1969
Shildon	1833	NER	LNER	1984
Swindon	1869	GWR	GWR	1962
Temple Mills	1896	GER	LNER	–
Walkergate	1902	NER	LNER	mid 1960s
York	1865	NER	LNER	mid 1960s

* The original wagon works were closed in 1965, but the work transferred to Doncaster Carriage Works.

British Railways Wagon Works

Ashford Wagon Works

Ashford Wagon Works was built in 1850 for the South Eastern Railway Company on a 32 acre site, primarily for the construction and repair of wagons. In addition to this work they built carriage underframes. By 1923, 827 members of staff were employed at the Works. Because of the mechanised manner of working, new wagons were produced quickly and efficiently and to a very high quality.

In 1962, the Wagon Works was amalgamated into the Locomotive Works, but because of the decrease in traffic and lack of contracts from overseas customers, closure came in 1982.

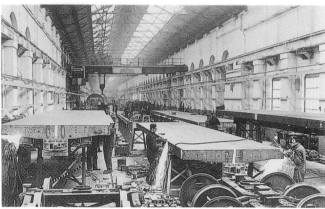

Ashford probably achieved its highest productivity levels in the years immediately preceding its closure, when in addition to its BR new-build programmes it was also engaged in large export orders. The long shops with their overhead crane facilities providing a perfect setting for bogie wagon construction. The abundance of jigs and welding plant, which can be seen here enabled the works to compete successfully in the very competitive export market.

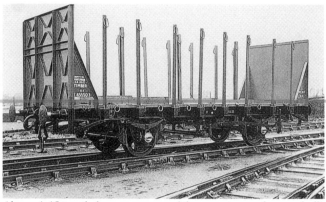

Above: A 15-ton timber wagon, one of the many types of wagon built for BR which are still in service.

Aerial view of the works seen in the later years of its BREL life. The corner of the main machine shop can just be seen on the left behind the propane gas storage tanks. The main construction shops are on the right hand side, with the repair shops immediately behind the traverser.

Barassie Wagon Works

Barassie Wagon Works was built in 1901 for the Glasgow & South Western Railway Company on a 22 acre site. It was the principal carriage and steel wagon works of the area. The site had in addition a further 40 acres which was only utilised during the Second World War for the repair of Spitfire aircraft which necessitated the building of a runway.

After 1929 carriage repairs were transferred to St Rollox and Barassie carried out only wagon and container repairs. The Works was finally closed in 1972.

Bromsgrove Wagon Works

Bromsgrove Wagon Works was built in 1840 for the Birmingham & Gloucester Railway Company on a 14 acre site as a wagon repair works. The Works were at the foot of the Lickey Incline on the Bristol to Birmingham line with a gradient of 1 in 37.7, the steepest in Britain.

The Works closed in 1964 with a staff of 400. All work was transferred to Derby Litchurch Lane Works.

HBA Hopper Wagons under repair at Barassie Works.

This aerial view of Bromsgrove Works, taken in 1925, is typical of many wagons works in that period trying to adapt workshops built in 1840 for their new commitments. The railway is the 'down' line to Bristol after leaving the Lickey incline. The works were originally built for the Birmingham & Gloucester Railway and were finally closed in September 1964.

Caerphilly Wagon Works

Caerphilly Carriage and Wagon Works was built in 1901 by the Rhymney Railway Company on a 6½ acre site. The final total of wagons was 1,200. Repairs were carried out and replacement stock was built, especially mineral brake vans and wagons. However in 1930 wagon work was transferred to Cardiff Cathays, followed by the end of carriage conversion work, and the gradual phasing out of carriage and wagon work. New carriage repair shops were later built at Caerphilly but no more wagon work was undertaken.

Cowlairs Wagon Works

Cowlairs Wagon Works was built in 1842 by the Edinburgh & Glasgow Railway Company on a 167 acre site. The Works was a combined locomotive, carriage and wagon works. Wagon repairs were split between heavy and light, but no new construction was undertaken. The Works closed in 1968 and the workload was transferred to St Rollox.

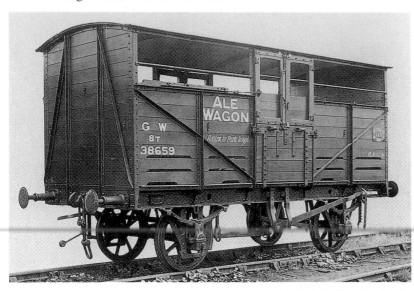

GWR Ale wagon – used as its name implies for carrying barrels of beer and very similar in design to the cattle wagons of that era. Note the specialised design of the side doors which allowed the bottom half to drop onto the horse drawn road dray and form a ramp to roll the barrels up.

(Swindon Railway Museum)

The GWR used telegraphic code names to denote their wagon stock whilst other railway companies tended to class them into general groups. In this particular case - MICA - indicates that timber bodied wagon No. 59791 was an end-ventilated van used for carrying meat.

(Swindon Railway Museum)

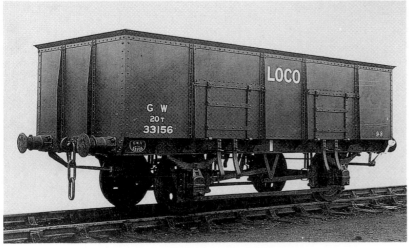

GWR Locomotive Coal wagon, a larger vehicle introduced into service in the 1920s to replace the old, smaller capacity, timber colliery wagons.

(Swindon Railway Museum)

Derby Wagon Works

Derby Carriage and Wagon Works was built in 1876 for the Midland Railway Company on a 128 acre site to undertake new building and repair of wagons and carriages. By the turn of the century, 180 new wagons were being completed per week. Before long it was possible to construct wagons on a progressive line basis from the basic materials to being ready for painting within seven hours. During 1949, 3,674 wagons were constructed in addition to over 13,000 mixed repairs.

In 1954, 1,800 people were employed in wagon construction and repair at Derby. Also during the 1950s, conversion work was being undertaken on wagons for the fitting of vacuum brakes which included contracts for outside firms. The Works also built 169 trailer cars for London Transport Executive.

In 1962 all new building ceased and repairs were cut back. The container building also ceased in 1979.

Above: Lifting a goods brake with two overhead cranes in the bay in the carriage lift shop, which was allocated to wagons too heavy or too long for the facilities in the actual wagon repair shop.

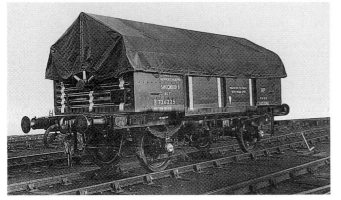

20-ton 'Shochood B' wagon built at Derby in 1962, as its name implies these wagons had built-in shock absorbers to protect the load during shunting operations etc.

(British Railways)

Below: 'Coil B' wagon built at Derby in 1963 with a tilt cover to protect the new steel coils from inclement weather.

(British Railways)

Three different builds of all-steel containers outside the container paint shop. In the late 1960s and early '70s Derby was heavily committed to building specialised types of containers for the private market, in addition to its BR workload. (Although classed as wagon activities the above were in reality done on the carriage side.)
(British Railways)

This plaque commemorates a fitter who started work at Derby when he was aged 13 and continued working there for 72 years, until he died at the age of 85!

Building of wooden wagons of 12-ton capacity at Derby Carriage and Wagon Works, during the period 1924-1930.

(BREL)

Doncaster Wagon Works

Doncaster Wagon Works was built in 1889 for the Great Northern Railway Company on a 32 acre site. Various wagon types were built – open, covered and refrigerated, for carrying machinery, timber, gas, oil, etc. In 1923 new building work stopped but repairs continued.

The Works closed in 1965 and wagon work was transferred to the carriage works.

Tank wagon barrel at Doncaster Carriage and Wagon Works.
(BREL)

The original wagon shops at Doncaster were sited some distance away from the locomotive and carriage works. When these shops were closed down, the wagon activity was moved into part of the carriage works, hence the rather grandiose appearance evident here. The conventional traverser in the foreground was subsequently replaced by the first hover-type traverser to be installed in the UK.

Earlestown Wagon Works

Earlestown Carriage and Wagon Works was built in 1853 on a 36 acre site for Jones & Potts, to be acquired by the London & North Western Railway Company in the same year. By 1901, 2,000 members of staff were employed with 4,000 wagons being constructed per year in addition to 13,000 heavy repairs and 200 horse-drawn vehicles built.

In 1924 mass production methods were introduced and during the first seven years, 19,540 standard wagons were produced. Wagon couplings were also manufactured in mass production methods.

In 1963 the Works was closed and the workload transferred to Horwich, along with many of the staff.

The frame for a new wagon prepared in 1926.
(National Railway Museum)

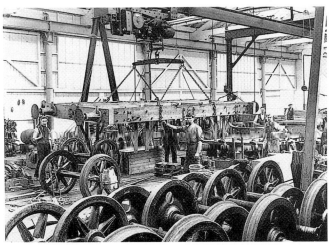

End-door open goods wagon under construction in 1950 at Earlestown Wagon Works, a period when the railways were trying to overcome the arrears of maintenance and shortfalls in new-build during the war years. Timber at this period was more readily available than steel, which was soon to replace these timber wagons. Note the pneumatic nut runners and drills, the forerunners of the vast range of powered hand tools available today.

(National Railway Museum)

Construction of cattle wagons in 1927 at Earlestown. Note how the timber underframe members have all been fully machined down to the last detail before assembly.

(National Railway Museum)

Eastleigh Wagon Works

Eastleigh Carriage and Wagon Works was built in 1891 by the London & South-Western Railway Company on a 54 acre site. The Works constructed new carriages and containers and repaired carriages, wagons and containers. By 1968 the repair work had been transferred to the locomotive works and the site was sold.

Repair of timber bodied containers and their flat wagons at Eastleigh in the late 1960s

Works at Eastleigh were first established by the London & South Western Railway in 1891 when the Carriage Works were transferred from Nine Elms. The Locomotive Works followed in 1910, with all activities being carried out in the former Locomotive Works in recent years having been reorganised for this purpose, following the closure of the former Carriage Works.

Faverdale Wagon Works

Faverdale Wagon Works was built in 1923 for the North Eastern Railway Company on a 60 acre site. It originally constructed 10,000 timber-framed wagons per year using ironwork details from Shildon. By 1949, 572 members of staff were employed at Faverdale and during this year 1,588 new wagons were built and 295 containers in addition to a large amount of carriage, wagon and container repairs. The first grain wagons built for any railway in Britain were constructed here.

In 1962 the Works closed after only 39 years.

Gorton Wagon Works

Gorton Carriage and Wagon Works were built in 1881 by the North Eastern Railway Company on a $5^3/_4$ acre site. Only light repairs to carriages and repairs to wagons and horse-drawn vehicles were undertaken. The Works were closed in 1965.

Horwich Wagon Works

Horwich Works started life as a Locomotive Works, built in 1887 for the Lancashire & Yorkshire Railway Company, covering a total area of 81 acres. However, all locomotive work ceased in 1963 when Earlestown Wagon Works closed and the workload was transferred to Horwich, which became purely a Wagon Works. However, this work also stopped in 1982 when Horwich Works itself was closed.

Inverurie Wagon Works

Inverurie Locomotive, Carriage and Wagon Works was built in 1903 for the Great North of Scotland Railway Company on a 15 acre site. The carriage and wagon work was very limited, employing only 240 people by 1947, with mostly light wagon repairs being undertaken. Because of the decrease in traffic, the Works closed on 31st December 1969.

Shildon Wagon Works

Shildon Wagon Works was built in 1833 for the Stockton & Darlington Railway Company on a 40 acre site. The Works started life as a Locomotive Works but later became a wagon works. It was the oldest main works and the largest British Rail wagon works.

During the Second World War, 54,000 tank trap shoes were manufactured at the Works. Shildon Wagon Works was modernised in 1962 to construct and repair British Rail wagons and later, for overseas companies. A variety of new designs were tested and manufactured at Shildon, for example the 'Presflo' cement wagons and Freightliner wagons. After the re-equipment of the Works in 1972, all drop-stamp forging was undertaken here for the whole of British Rail. Over 11,000 'Merry-go-round' coal hoppers were built here between 1965 and 1982. However, by this time the requirement for new British Rail freight stock had so greatly diminished due to lower costs of road transportation that Shildon was closed in 1984. At that time, 12,000 people were employed at the Works. In 1980

the Works had been the location for the Stockton & Darlington Railway 150th anniversary celebrations and was host to many locomotives and people for the week-long activities.

The world's first public railway, the 1825 Stockton & Darlington, ran in this area, so it is appropriate to include here a wagon standing on fish bellied track and on display in the grounds of Shildon Works.

General view of the drop stamp and forge, a vital constituent part of the works production. The furnaces at Shildon were all oil-fired from a centralised storage tank.

(British Railways)

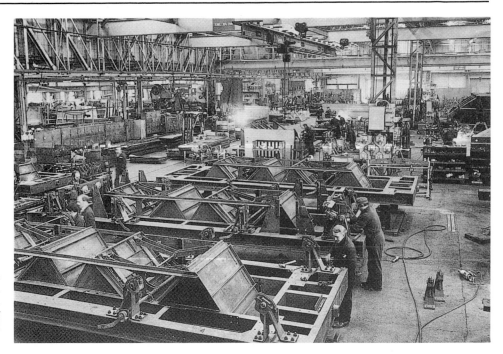

Assembling a 26-ton high-capacity coal wagon in the then new construction bay in 1968. Shildon manufactured no less than eleven thousand of these wagons for the merry-go-round services.

A completed HBA 40-ton coal wagon, No. 360219, built at Shildon Works.

Construction of high-sided wooden wagons in 1910. The foreman can be identified from his workers by his bowler hat, a traditional badge of office common to all works. The heating and lighting facilities were most primitive when compared with modern day standards.

(National Railway Museum)

Top Left: A section of the wagon repair shop at Shildon in BR days.

Top Right: A high-capacity wagon in the brake and lift shop.

Left: Building of high-sided wooden wagons at Shildon Works.
(National Railway Museum)

Below Left: Fitting of brake pipework and suspension gear to the underside of steel wagons in 1970.
(British Railways)

Below Right: Timber storage shed for new wagons.
(National Railway Museum)

Swindon Wagon Works

Swindon Carriages and Wagon Works was built in 1869 by the Great Western Railway Company on 137 acres. Wagon building was a very important part of work undertaken from very early days, including standard and experimental vehicles. A wagon repair shop was built in 1880. Many specialised wagons were built, including low-loading types, gun trucks, refrigerated vans, ventilated vans and circus vans. The Carriage and Wagon shop was closed in the 1960s.

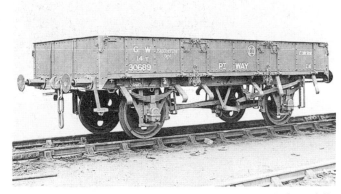

GWR drop-sided open wagon (in service for a long period) specially built for the Civil Engineers Department to carry ballast for track repairs and renewals.

(Swindon Railway Museum)

Aerial view taken by the Bristol Aeroplane Company in 1922 of the original wagon shops at Swindon, probably the largest concentrated repair unit in the UK. In 1967 these activities were all transferred to the locomotive works.

'DAMO. A' - GWR goods van with a long wheel base of 19 ft, used for special loads such as furniture. Note the end-loading door with its drop flap in addition to the conventional side doors.

(Swindon Railway Museum)

Right: Shock-absorbing van used for carrying fragile material, such as glass and china. The helical springs can be seen below the doorway which dampened out buffing and drawgear shock loads.

(Swindon Railway Museum)

Below: In addition to conventional new building, all Works had to cater for special conversions. A typical example is *Prometheus*, which was converted at Swindon in 1976 for use as a laboratory research vehicle to study pantograph displacement.

(H. R. Roberts)

Temple Mills Wagon Works

Temple Mills Wagon Works was built in 1896 for the Great Eastern Railway Company on a 24 acre site to repair wagons. By 1949, 400 members of staff were employed. Several prototypes were developed here including wagons for the previous Channel Tunnel project. The Works closed in 1984 due to the decrease in workload.

Walkergate Wagon Works

Walkergate Carriage and Wagon Works was built in 1902 for the North Eastern Railway Company on a 14 acre site to repair carriages and wagons. Fire destroyed much of the stock in August 1918. In 1949 508 people were employed here. The Works closed in the 1960s and work was transferred to Shildon and York.

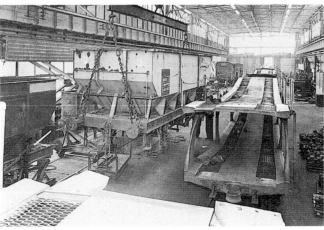

Facilities were developed at Temple Mills to maintain the fleets of car transporter train sets, such as that on the right. The hopper wagon on the left is being lifted off the temporary bogies on which it has been repaired, to be carried down the shop for re-wheeling.

Vacuum repair layout, Walkergate Wagon Works. After repair each cylinder had to be tested individually under load for a specified maximum leak-test measured over a time base, hence the clock faces at the side of each of the cylinders on test.

(H. R. Roberts)

The wagon lifting bay at Temple Mills illustrating the mixed nature of the workloads, with timber-bodied 12-ton covered goods vans intermingled with steel open wagons and bulk cement wagons.

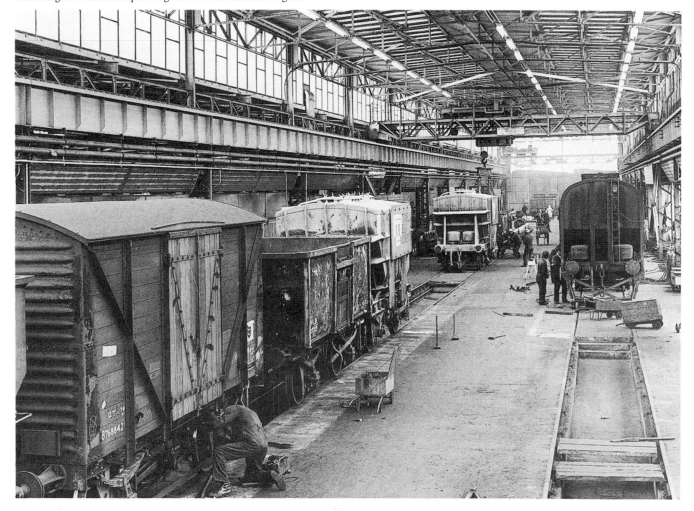

Walkergate Works, on the right of this photograph, were sited adjacent to the North Tyneside third-rail electric commuter line and had a workload which mostly arose from the wagons involved in the local coal and steel industries.

(British Railways)

Wagon machine shop, York, at the turn of the century.
(National Railway Museum)

York Wagon Works

York Wagon Works was built in 1865 for the North Eastern Railway Company on a 17 acre site to repair wagons and horseboxes. The carriage works was not built until 1884. By 1949, 801 members of staff were employed, repairing 12,963 freight vehicles, a good mix of light and heavy repairs. By this time container repairs were also undertaken. The Works closed in the 1960s and many staff moved to York Carriage Works.

5
BR Works Training Schools

Origin of Scheme

Following a conversation between Sir Harold Hartley, FRS, Vice-President, and Sir William Stanier, FRS Chief Mechanical Engineer, of the London, Midland & Scottish Railway Co. late in 1940, the latter invited the author, E.J. Larkin, at that time Assistant Works Superintendent of the Derby Locomotive Works to investigate the possibility of developing a training scheme. This was to be devised to cover Apprentices, whether of the trade or engineering type, which combined both practical and theoretical work as a full time course prior to the Apprentices being placed on productive work in the Workshops. Provision was to be made in the training scheme to include such lecturing in Workshop practices and associated subjects as might be considered desirable. The underlying idea was for a scheme to be developed with a view to its introduction on the cessation of hostilities.

Early in 1941 the Investigator submitted his Report, a copy of which was sent by the Company to the Rt Hon. Herwald Ramsbotham, President of the Board of Education. The proposals covered all the Main Works of the LMS, and provided for the establishment of seven Works Training Schools and the inclusion therein of several novel features. It was to be a 12-months full-time course. Not the least noteworthy was the recommendation that the Board of Education should be invited to co-operate and allow full time lecturers under the local Education Authorities to visit the Schools and lecture in certain specified subjects, leaving other subjects to be covered by Railway appointed staff. Another interesting proposal was that all the principal Workshop trades should be covered in the School – an arrangement not to be found elsewhere. It was scientifically planned that the Workshop equipment and classroom accommodation would be such that they were in use at all times, thus helping to ensure animation and a true workshop atmosphere.

On 19th June 1941, the Investigator was presented to the President of the Board of Education, when the latter said he was impressed with the proposals and would give them his full support. Following this, the Investigator was invited to meet the LMS Directors and explain how the scheme would operate.

Authority was subsequently obtained for the establishment of a Works Training School at Derby Locomotive Works. It was officially opened by Sir Robert Burrows, Chairman of the LMS in December 1947, and, dependent upon the results achieved, consideration was to be given to the provision of similar facilities at each of the other six Main Works of the LMS.

Shortly after Nationalisation of the Transport Industry in January 1948, members of the British Transport Commission, together with the Labour and Establishment members of the five Executives set up by the Commission, visited Derby to inspect the Works Training School in operation. Following this visit, the British Transport Commission, in their report entitled Staff Training and Education, recommended that the general pattern of practical and theoretical training at the School at Derby should be developed and extended to the larger Workshop centres of all the Executives wherever practicable.

Within a few years the LMR had a total of seven Works Training Schools, namely Derby Locomotive, Derby Carriage and Wagon, Crewe, Earlestown, St Rollox, Horwich and Wolverton Works.

After Nationalisation the British Transport Commission approved the establishment of similar training schools on the other Regions at the Works of Doncaster, Eastleigh, Swindon and York. When completed there were no fewer than eleven Works Training Schools on British Railways. Subsequently London Transport provided a similar Apprentice Training School at their Acton Works, and for good measure, Rolls-Royce, Derby visited the well-established Locomotive Works Training School and set up a corresponding one on their own property.

In 1948, the year of the Nationalisation of the Railways, there was a total of 11,000 apprentices employed in the Main Works and various maintenance depots under the Control of other railway technical departments.

Two trainees 'casting' under the watchful eye of the instructor.

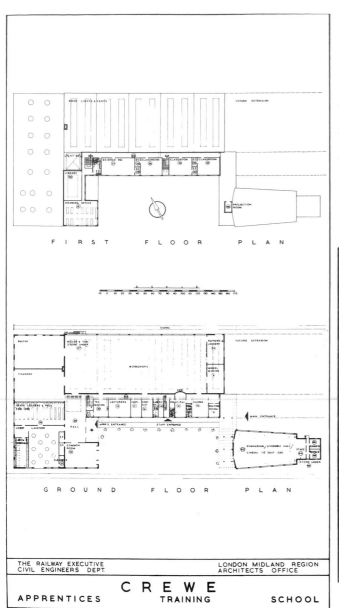

THE RAILWAY EXECUTIVE
CIVIL ENGINEERS DEPT.

LONDON MIDLAND REGION
ARCHITECTS OFFICE

CREWE
APPRENTICES   TRAINING   SCHOOL

Left: Crewe Works Training School Plan. The School was officially opened on 22nd September 1953.

Below: Apprentice fitters valve setting, Erecting Shop, Horwich Works, 1959.

Bottom: General view of the Works Training School, Horwich, 1963.

Above: A general view of the Works Training School, Crewe.

Left: General view of the Works Training School, Doncaster.

Classroom view of the BR Training School, Derby.

Entrance to the Works Training School at York, 1972.

Below: The BR Engineering Training School, Derby, for professional and technical staff and workshop supervisory staff. A new wing was added for Diesel Instruction in 1954.

(British Railways)

Workshop view of the BR Training School, Derby showing a railcar rig with the inner wheel of a bogie incorporating final drive. This axle can be rotated by engine drive, and simulation of road speed through the gearbox can be obtained up to a maximum of 70mph.

General view of the Works Training School, Swindon, 1965.

Schoolboys and Senior Students Own Exhibition, Horticultural Halls, Westminster, 31st December 1953 to 13th January 1954.

Twenty apprentice trainees, chosen from both the Locomotive and Carriage and Wagon Works Training Schools at Derby, went to London to demonstrate their skills, taking with them their own equipment, including lathes, smiths' hearth, crucible furnace, benches and hand tools.

The boys worked in two teams of ten each. Whilst one team was working at the Exhibition, the others went on pre-arranged visits such as the Tower of London, Houses of Parliament, also local engineering works and Locomotive Running Sheds.

The supervisors on the Stand were chosen from the instruction staffs of the two Derby Training Schools.

6
Wartime Products in the Railway Workshops

The utilisation of the Railway Companies' workshops in the First World War, 1914–1918, and in the Second World War,1939-1945, makes fascinating history.

In both wars full consideration was given to many items of Government work which could be manufactured, or repaired, in several of the railway workshops. These included the manufacture of armoured tanks, aeroplane fuselages and wings, ambulance trains, breakdown trains, shells, mobile kitchens, and a vast variety of wartime components.

Technical staff in the Drawing Offices, and highly skilled artisan staff in the Workshops, undertook outstanding wartime jobs. To quote just one example, the 'Covenanter' tank, was designed in the Derby LMSR Locomotive Drawing Office, and they were built, tested, and handed over to the Army at Crewe Locomotive Works.

The Vulcan Foundry designed the 'Matilda' tank, and 406 were built at Horwich Works. Other tanks were designed and built at different centres.

A noticeable feature of several of the railway workshops in the two World Wars was the employment of women who were trained to undertake work normally performed by men.

12in Howitzers mounted on four-wheel bogie railway trucks built towards the end of the First World War, after which they were placed in store. At the beginning of the Second World War 23 of them went into Derby Carriage and Wagon Works to be renovated; the first being sent off to its destination on 16th April 1940, and the last completed in December.

Final stages of Typhoon Wing Production at Derby Carriage and Wagon Works. Approximately 1,000 pairs were completed by March 1944.

The women showed themselves to be remarkably adaptable to the heavy engineering work dealt with in railway workshops and numbers of them displayed such interest and versatility that they undertook really high class work including:

Turning of piston valve heads and rings.
Grinding of motion pins.
High grade fitting work.
Electric and oxy-acetylene welding.
Crane driving.
Operation of power hammers.
Examination, cleaning, oiling and greasing of carriages and wagons.

Matilda Tank: designed by the Vulcan Foundry. Horwich Works built 406 between 1939 and February 1943.

Below: 17-pounder anti-tank carriage and gun – a modern weapon with high muzzle velocity and semi-automatic cartridge ejecting gear. 250 of the carriages for these guns had most of the material prepared for them and were assembled in Derby Locomotive Works. Welded construction was adopted extensively in the design of the carriages. Output commenced in October 1942 being amongst the foremost produced in this country. The 250th and the last carriage left the Works in July 1943. Spare assemblies and components were also manufactured for this gun carriage, including 750 saddles, 526 cradles, 2,400 semi-automatice gears and 730 training bases.

Below: In the First World War the Midland Railway 0-6-0 freight locomotive No. 2717 was loaned to the British Army in 1915 and was isolated in No-Man's Land for many months. It was eventually captured by the Germans and restored by them to working order. The dome cover suffered many bullets and the photograph shows the neatness of the repairs undertaken by the Germans. At the end of the war the locomotive was returned to Derby Locomotive Works and retained for a while as a museum piece.

7

Some Notable Occasions

The author has provided half a dozen interesting occasions from personal involvement.

King George V in the wheel turning and balancing section of the Wheel Shop at Swindon, 28th April 1924.
(H. R. Roberts)

King George V and Queen Mary visiting the casting of a welcome message in the Iron Foundry at Swindon Locomotive Works, 28th April 1924.
(H. R. Roberts)

King George V and Queen Mary watching a seamstress at Swindon Works making a luggage rack netting.
(H. R. Roberts)

Locomotive No. 4082 *Windsor Castle*, at the head of the Royal Train taking their Majesties back to Windsor. The King drove the train himself from the Works to Swindon station.
(H. R. Roberts)

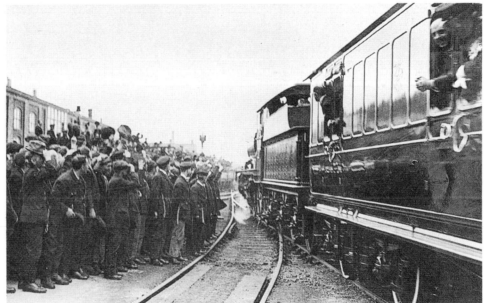

'Castle' class 4-6-0 No. 4082 *Windsor Castle* standing outside 'A' Shop, Swindon Works ready to haul King George V's funeral train, with the men who had prepared her for this Royal occasion.

(H. R. Roberts)

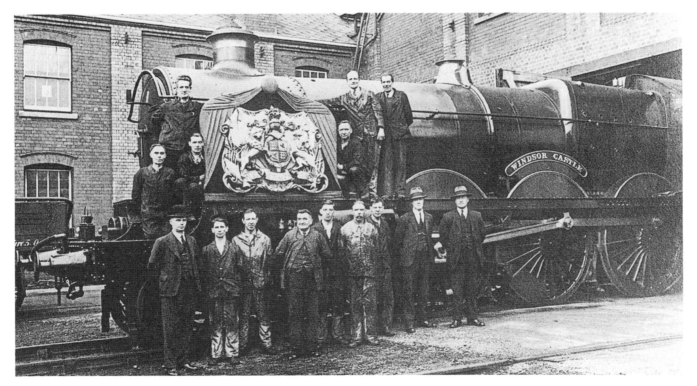

King George VI and Queen Elizabeth (now the Queen Mother) on the footplate of SR 4-6-0 No. 850 *Lord Nelson* during a visit to Ashford Works in 1926, with Sir Edward Baring, the Chairman, Mr R. E. L. Maunsell, Chief Mechanical Engineer and Driver Francis.

Right & Below: Exhibiting the *Royal Scot* locomotive, No. 6100, one of 50 4-6-0 passenger locomotives built in Derby Locomotive Works in 1928. The author was the demonstrator in charge of the locomotive when it was on exhibition in different cities and towns in the following order: Manchester, Birmingham, Bradford, Sheffield, Liverpool, Derby, London, Leeds, Preston and Crewe. This tour was followed by an equally successful tour in Scotland, the total number of visitors being around 200,000. The highest attendance on any one day was made at Sheffield when 7,259 visitors paid for admission. On one occasion there were two ladies together. One said to the other "I've been on the locomotive. I went into the cab and came out through the smokebox." Some flue tubes to be sure! All monies received were handed over to the local hospitals and Bradford dedicated a cot called the 'Royal Scot Cot'.

Sir Joseph Stamp (later Lord Stamp) was appointed President of the LMS Executive in 1926, controlling approximately 240,000 staff, and the following year he also became Chairman of the LMS – a dual position. The photograph shows him on *Lion* at Wavertree Park, Liverpool, during the Liverpool & Manchester Railway Centenary celebrations in 1930. Lloyd George once described him as the greatest living economist. Sadly, in 1941 during the Second World War, an enemy bomb dropped on his home shelter at Watford and he, his wife and eldest son were all killed.

The *Lion* locomotive, accepted throughout the world as the oldest locomotive in working order, following restoration in Crewe Locomotive Works, being handed over to the Liverpool Engineering Society in 1930. *Lion* was built by Todd, Kitson & Laird, Leeds in 1838.

On the extreme left of the photograph is W. Brudenell, LMS Press Officer. Next to him is S. J. Symes, Assistant Chief Mechanical Engineer. The five next to him are senior officers of the LMS and include Ashton Davies, Chief Commercial Officer, LMS, and Chairman of the Centenary Organising Committee, and H. P. M. Beames, Works Manager of Crewe Locomotive Works.

On the extreme right of the photograph is the author, E. J. Larkin, representing Sir Henry Fowler, KBE, Chief Mechanical Engineer of the London, Midland & Scottish Railway who was on a mission to the USA. The six next to him are officers of the Liverpool Engineering Society. During the restoration, the author was in contact with J. G. H. Warren, author of the classic book *A Century of Locomotive Building by Robert Stephenson & Co 1823-1923*, published in 1923.

Above: Sir Nigel Gresley standing by the A4 Pacific locomotive No. 4498, named after him in 1937 at King's Cross Depot.

Left: The author making an introductory speech at the official opening of the first Works Training School on British Railways, by Sir Robert Burrows, Chairman of the LMSR on 4th December 1947.

Below: Diesel-electric main line locomotive No. 10000. It was designed jointly by H. G. Ivatt and the English Electric Company and was built in Derby in 1947 to be followed by her twin, No. 10001 in 1948, the year of Nationalisation. When the former made her first trip from Derby Locomotive Works to Marylebone for inspection by Lord Robertson, Chairman and Member of the British Transport Commission on 16th December 1947, H. G. Ivatt invited the author to travel with him on the footplate. This was quite an occasion and the author remembers saying to him that the locomotive cab was so comfortable that the biggest job for the driver would be staying awake!

Above: The entry of BR Standard Class 5 4-6-0 No. 73000 into traffic on 12th April 1951. Seventh from left is the locomotive designer, R. A. Riddles OBE, member of BR Executive for Mechanical, Electrical and Signal Engineering. The author, E. J. Larkin, is on the extreme right of the twelve well-known, senior railway officers.

Right: HRH The Duke of Edinburgh with T. C. Baynton Hughes, Special Projects Officer, inspecting BR Standard Class 9F 2-10-0 heavy freight locomotive No. 92220 at the Exhibition of Locomotives and Rolling Stock at Marylebone Goods Station on 12th May 1961, arranged by the BTC to mark the occasion of the Golden Jubilee of the Institution of Locomotive Engineers. No. 92220 was specially named *Evening Star,* the last steam locomotive to be built for BR, and a product of Swindon Locomotive Works (Western Region) and the 999th BR Standard locomotive. This locomotive has been preserved and continues to work steam-hauled special trains.

Below: Bulleid Pacific No. 34051 *Winston Churchill* conveying the funeral train of Sir Winston at Staines, 30th January 1965.

(J. G. Click)

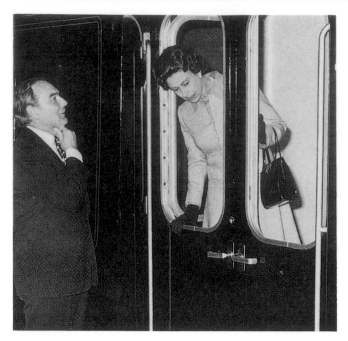

Queen Elizabeth II and Prince Philip in their new Royal train built at Wolverton Works, Buckinghamshire, in 1988 having just been handed the key for the Royal Coaches by Sir Peter Parker, then Chairman of British Rail. Compartments in the new Royal Train are spartan compared to the unashamed luxury of the one used by Queen Victoria. The lavishly decorated compartments with silk and satin furnishings have given way to carriages which are elegant, but plane and functional, with full air-conditioning.

Most of the £500,000 was spent on refurbishing eight 1972 InterCity prototype coaches of which £120,000 was spent on two new Royal saloons, fitted out to meet the requirements of the Queen and the Duke. The Queen's saloon has a lounge, bedroom and bathroom, together with a bedroom and bathroom for her dresser. The ceiling panels are white melamine, and the principal wall finishing is a cream PVC wall pattern. The carpet throughout is slate blue, and both the bedroom and lounge have subdued lighting. Blue is the main theme throughout, with the blue carpet, a pale blue easy chair and blue and white curtains. Some prints of the first Royal Train journeys by Queen Victoria were selected for hanging in the Queen's Saloon. Prince Philip's carriage is slightly smaller because it has a kitchen fitting with a shower instead of a bath.

Engine Driver John Drayton, located at Newport, Ebbw Junction Depot, Wales, was presented with a special award (in August 1959) for having made 1,000 successful suggestions. The event attracted attention at the time and his name appeared in the *Guinness Book of Records*. He was clearly a man who kept his eyes open as he went about his work, and many of his suggestions were related to points of safety on the line, or on the designs of the locomotives which he drove, to improve safety and the comfort and convenience of the footplate staff. He had a book published entitled *Life in the Valleys*. From left to right in the photograph are R. L. Charlesworth, Commercial Manager, Western Region, and Chairman of the Western Region Suggestions Committee, H.E.A. White, Motive Power Superintendent, Western Region, J. R. Hammond, General Manager, Western Region, John Drayton, Engine Driver, and the author, E. J. Larkin, Director of Work Study, British Transport Commission.

The final batch of locomotives to be produced by the Locomotive Works at Swindon compised 20 eight-coupled diesel-hydraulic shunting locomotives for export to Kenya's metre gauge system. They were built to a Hunslet design, and incorporated a Rolls-Royce DV8 TCF engine of 525bhp driving through a Voith transmission. The turbo transmission had a separate torque converter for each direction (the driver could go straight from forward into reverse or visa-versa, a facility British Rail never had). On 3rd November 1979, the first of these locomotives, KR No. 4716, was on display to the Press. Sadly, this represented the last of the line of so many fine locomotives to be produced at Swindon, chosen by Brunel in 1839 to be the main locomotive headquarters of the Great Western Railway. These locomotives weighed 53 tonnes with a maximum axle load of 13.5 tonnes and a maximum starting tractive effort with 30% adhesion was 15,900 Kg. The minimum curve negotiable was 88 metres.

8
Universal Machine Tools in Carriage and Wagon Works

A book on Railway Workshops would not be complete without a brief introduction to some of the machines and techniques which were common to most of them. Because of the identical nature of these techniques between works no effort has been made to identify the actual picture locations as each one is intended as a representative of national practices.

Timber was the most common material in use for nearly a century so it is perhaps the best starting point.

Logs had first to be cut up into slabs by huge saws such as this where the log was fed into the blade at a speed related to the hardness of the wood and the girth of the tree. The majority of band saws were horizontal not vertical as illustrated. After the timber slabs had been seasoned they were then ready for further machining. Only the major works were equipped with log saws so they had the responsibility of supplying sister works with timber ready for final machining.

(National Railway Museum)

The high speed router was a common feature in all works and was used to shape components. A copy spindle followed a timber pattern whilst the cutting tool shaped the actual timber component underneath. In a later era these machines were successfully adapted for machining aluminium.

(H. R. Roberts)

Machining timber produced vast quantities of sawdust and chippings which, when tipped on land-fill sites, presented unacceptable fire risks. The obvious solution was to burn it in life expired locomotive boilers and raise steam for use in the works. The main sawdust extraction pipe from the sawmill entered the cyclone at the top of the picture and the segregated wood waste either dropped into the boiler firebox housed in the building or excess flow could be diverted into the wagon.

(H. R. Roberts)

The 'backroom' equipment which made the previous plant so efficient. The boiler is in the right foreground and leading from it are a water bath and cyclone dust extractor to clean the exhaust gases before they reached the chimney. Instrumentation to monitor smoke density and effective combustion levels can be seen around the chimney stack. The asbestos sheets provided a fire-proof store for the sawdust and chippings.

(H. R. Roberts)

This railway works combined sawdust and refuse burning plant became the prototype for many municipal authorities who copied it to dispose of their household waste. The sawdust and chippings stored above the ceiling were fed into the firebox via the chute and two rotary sprindlers above the open side-loading doors. The mixed nature of rubbish and waste can be seen around the bottom of tne photograph. The actual waste heat boiler is in the right background.

(H. R. Roberts)

A long time before fork lifts and other mechanical handling machines were in common use in British industry the railways had developed their own in-house systems. The three-wheeled articulated tractor illustrated here had an elevating platform which lifted the stillage legs clear of the ground for transhipment. It will be noted that stillages in other photographs were compatible to the same system.

(H. R. Roberts)

The reconditioning of leaf springs was a basic necessity in all works and the plant above is typical for a carriage repair works up to the 1960s, after which this activity was centralised into a few centres.

(H. R. Roberts)

Another activity common to all works was the necessity to remove accumulated dirt and grease from components requiring refurbishing, commonly referred to as 'boshing'. The bosh in the photograph is of the tunnel variety, where, in this case, axleboxes are being transversed through a compartment in which they are sprayed with high pressure jets of hot caustic water. Larger boshes were capable of accommodating a bogie complete with all its rigging.

(H. R. Roberts)

After carriage wheels had been turned on their treads it was necessary to 'balance' them in the same manner in which motor car tyres are serviced to avoid any out-of-balance load affecting the smoothness of the ride. Machines such as this were installed in all carriage works. The wheel set revolved on its journals which were supported on rollers. The shaft connecting the machine to the wheel set can be clearly seen. A read-out on the console details the out-of-balance weight and defined angle which the operator rectified by fixing balance plates to each wheel.

(H. R. Roberts)

The ubiquitous screw cutting machine was a necessity in even the smallest works or depot. This twin-headed model is cutting threads on forgings from a sister works.

(H. R. Roberts)

Because of the repetitive nature of most of the work it was possible to develop jigs to obtain the maximum potential from machines. In this instance coupler support pins are being gang milled just within the maximum permissible traverse limitations of the table. Note the stillage system and tractor haulage in operation in an era prior to the last war.

(H. R. Roberts)

Another 'maid-of-all-works' was the manually-operated capstan lathe, a very versatile machine which could meet any demand for pins, bushes and other turned components. The bar stock was fed through the headstock and the capstan tool post together with the front and back tool slides covered any combination of reducing bases, screw threading etc.

(H. R. Roberts)

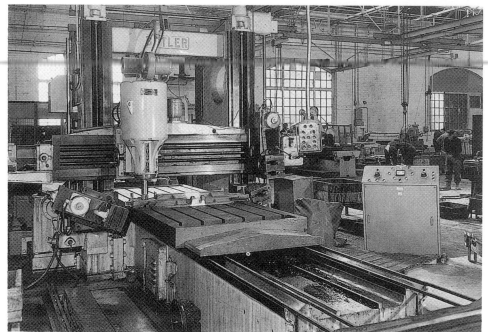

All the larger works had several planing machines where the article to be machined was clamped to a reciprocating table moving past a fixed cutting tool. Metal removal was a slow process because the tool only cut on the forward stroke. Rapid developments in machine tools after the last war made such machines obsolete, but the cost of replacement on a national scale was prohibitive. Alternative solutions were found, in this particular case a modern planomill head has been 'grafted' onto an old fashioned planing machine which gave all the advantages of the new generation of machine tools at a fraction of their cost.

(H. R. Roberts)

Oil reclamation was practised by all constituent companies prior to Nationalisation. This photograph shows part of the GWR oil reclamation plant located at Swindon early this century. In recent years it has become the practice to delegate this work to private specialist companies.

One of the 1970's generation of numerically controlled machines drilling an aluminium carriage door casting.

(H. R. Roberts)

The ultimate replacement machine for the manually operated capstan lathe. This battery of modern capstan lathes is fully automatic and one operator can service three machines.

(J. R. Staples)

A modern 'roll-on' type wheel lathe for bringing worn tyres back to their required profile. Astronomically expensive, they can do the work of three of the older models and are fully equipped with digital read-outs and other facilities to maximise output.

(J. R. Staples)

Axles which break in service have been a nightmare to railway engineers since the very early days, but it was not until the early 1960s that technology was developed which permitted ultrasonic scanning of axles to detect internal flaws.

This photograph shows a flaw in an axle which was invisible from the exterior. The dark portion is the flawed area, the crystalline area is virgin steel exposed when the axle was deliberately broken at the suspected flaw point.

(H. R. Roberts)

Ultrasonic flaw detector in operation. The probe which the operator is holding in his left hand is transmitting ultrasonic waves through the axle. If there is no flaw the display tube gives a straight line, any flaw shows up as a blip. Grease on the axle ensure good surface connection.

(H.R. Roberts)

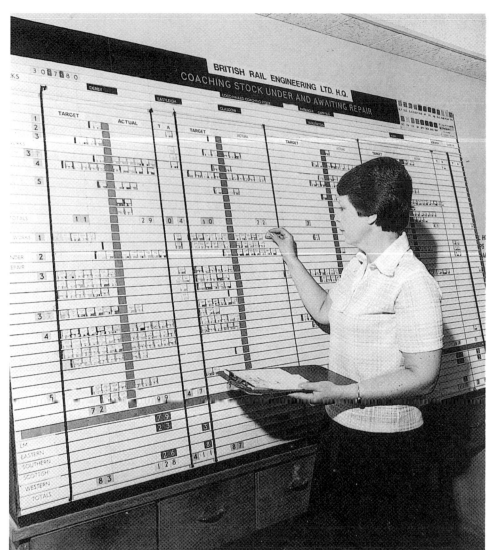

Each card on the control board illustrated gives all relevant information on one vehicle and its position on the board defines its actual location in the works. Any vehicle deviating from its planned repair time schedule is highlighted in red. The pool of vehicles on the right hand side were allocated priority of input in accordance with the available balance of labour shown on the adjacent labour leading board.

(H. R. Roberts)

Variations in trade workloads on individual carriage repairs necessitate a tight control on vehicle input sequence to avoid any one trade bottlenecking the others. Prior to the mid-1960s it was possible to delegate this authority to the supervisors until it became obvious that the growing complexity of modern stock was creating difficulties beyond their capacity, so repair control centres were established.

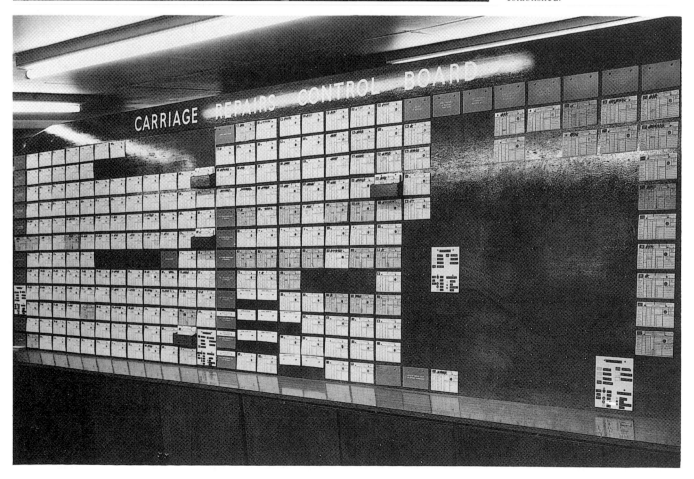

Appendix I

Order in which BR's Main Works were built.

Order in which built	Year built	Location of works	Owning Company in 1923	Class of work undertaken
1	1833	Shildon	LNER	Wagons
2	1838	Wolverton	LMSR	Carriages
3	1840	Brighton	SR	Locomotives
4	1840	Bromsgrove	LMSR	Wagons
5	1840	Derby	LMSR	Locomotives
6	1842	Cowlairs	LNER	Locomotives, Carriages and Wagons
7	1842	Swindon	GWR	Locomotives
8	1843	Crewe	LMSR	Locomotives
9	1847	Ashford	SR	Locomotives
10	1847	Stratford	LNER	Locomotives
11	1847	Stratford	LNER	Carriages
12	1849	Gorton	LNER	Locomotives
13	1850	Ashford	SR	Wagons
14	1850	Bow	LMSR	Locomotives
15	1853	Doncaster	LNER	Locomotives
16	1853	Doncaster	LNER	Carriages
17	1853	Earlestown	LMSR	Wagons
18	1855	Wolverhampton	GWR	Locomotives
19	1856	St Rollox	LMSR	Locomotives
20	1856	St Rollox	LMSR	Carriages
21	1856	Kilmarnock	LMSR	Locomotives
22	1863	Darlington	LNER	Locomotives
23	1865	York	LNER	Wagons
24	1869	Swindon	GWR	Carriages and Wagons
25	1876	Derby Litchurch Lane	LMSR	Carriages and Wagons
26	1881	Gorton	LNER	Carriages and Wagons
27	1884	York	LNER	Carriages
28	1887	Horwich	LMSR	Locomotives and Wagons
29	1888	Lancing	SR	Carriages
30	1889	Doncaster	LNER	Wagons
31	1891	Eastleigh	SR	Carriages
32	1896	Temple Mills	LNER	Wagons
33	1899	Caerphilly	GWR	Locomotives
34	1901	Barassie	LMSR	Wagons
35	1901	Caerphilly	GWR	Carriages and Wagons
36	1902	Walkergate	LNER	Carriages and Wagons
37	1903	Inverurie	LNER	Locomotives, Carriages and Wagons
38	1909	Eastleigh	SR	Locomotives
39	1923	Faverdale	LNER	Wagons

Appendix II

Railway companies amalgamated to form the four main-line companies in 1923.

Great Western Railway Company
Constituent companies (7)
Barry Railway Company
Cambrian Railways Company
Cardiff Railway Company
Great Western Railway Company
Rhymney Railway Company
Taff Vale Railway Company
Alexandra (Newport & South Wales) Docks & Railway Company

Subsidiary companies (26)
Brecon & Merthyr Tydfil Junction Railway Company
Burry Port & Gwendreath Valley Railway Company
Cleobury Mortimer & Ditton Priors Light Railway Company
Didcot, Newbury & Southampton Railway Company
Exeter Railway Company
Forest of Dean Central Railway Company
Gwendreath Valleys Railway Company
Lampeter, Aberayron & New Quay Light Railway Company
Liskeard & Looe Railway Company
Llanelly & Mynydd Mawr Railway Company
Mawddy Railway Company
Midland & South Western Junction Railway Company
Neath & Brecon Railway Company
Penarth Extension Railway Company
Penarth Harbour, Dock & Railway Company
Port Talbot Railway & Docks Company
Princetown Railway Company
Rhondda & Swansea Bay Railway Company
Ross & Monmouth Railway Company
South Wales Mineral Railway Company
Teign Valley Railway Company
Vale of Glamorgan Railway Company
Van Railway Company
Welshpool & Llanfair Light Railway Company
West Somerset Railway Company
Wrexham & Ellesmere Railway Company

London, Midland & Scottish Railway Company
Constituent companies (8)
Caledonian Railway Company
Furness Railway Company
Glasgow & South Western Railway Company
Highland Railway Company
Lancashire & Yorkshire Railway Company
London & North Western Railway Company
Midland Railway Company
North Staffordshire Railway Company

Subsidiary companies (27)
Arbroath & Forfar Railway Company
Brechin & Edzell District Railway Company
Callander & Oban Railway Company
Cathcart District Railway Company
Charnwood Forest Railway Company
Cleator & Workington Junction Railway Company
Cockermouth, Keswick & Penrith Railway Company
Dearne Valley Railway Company

Dornoch Light Railway Company
Dundee & Newtyle Railway Company
Harborne Railway Company
Killin Railway Company
Knott End Railway Company
Lanarkshire & Ayrshire Railway Company
Leek & Manifold Light Railway Company
Maryport & Carlisle Railway Company
Mold & Denbigh Junction Railway Company
North & South Western Junction Railway Company
North London Railway Company
Portpatrick & Wigtownshire Joint Committee
Shropshire Union Railways & Canal Company
Solway Junction Railway Company
Stratford-upon-Avon & Midland Junction Railway Company
Tottenham & Forest Gate Railway Company
Wick & Lybster Light Railway Company
Wirral Railway Company
Yorkshire Dales Railway (Skipton to Grassington) Company

London & North Eastern Railway Company
Constituent companies (7)
Great Central Railway Company
Great Eastern Railway Company
Great Northern Railway Company
Great North of Scotland Railway Company
Hull & Barnsley Railway Company
North British Railway Company
North Eastern Railway Company

Subsidiary companies (26)
Brackenhill Light Railway Company
Colne Valley & Halstead Railway Company
East & West Yorkshire Union Railway Company
East Lincolnshire Railway Company
Edinburgh & Bathgate Railway Company
Forcett Railway Company
Forth & Clyde Junction Railway Company
Gifford & Garvald Railway Company
Great North of England, Clarence & Hartlepool Junction Railway Company
Horncastle Railway Company
Humber Commercial Railway & Dock Company
Kilsyth & Bonnybridge Railway Company
Lauder Light Railway Company
London & Blackwell Railway Company
Manfield Railway Company
Mid-Suffolk Light Railway Company
Newburgh & North Fife Railway Company
North Lindsey Light Railways Company
Nottingham & Grantham Railway & Canal Company
Nottingham Joint Station Committee
Nottingham Suburban Railway Company
Seaford & Sefton Junction Railway Company
Sheffield District Railway Company
South Yorkshire Junction Railway Company
Stamford & Essendine Railway Company
West Riding Railway Committee

Southern Railway Company

Constituent companies (5)
London & South Western Railway Company
London, Brighton & South Coast Railway Company
London, Chatham & Dover Railway Company
South Eastern Railway Company
South Eastern & Chatham Railway Companies Managing Committee

Subsidiary companies (14)
Bridgwater Railway Company
Brighton & Dyke Railway Company
Freshwater Yarmouth & Newport (Isle of Wight) Railway Company
Hayling Railways Company
Isle of Wight Railway Company
Isle of Wight Central Railway Company
Lee-on-the-Solent Railway Company
London & Greenwich Railway Company
Mid-Kent Railway (Bromley to St Mary Cray) Company
North Cornwall Railway Company
Plymouth & Dartmoor Railway Company
Plymouth, Devonport & South Western Junction Railway Company
Sidmouth Railway Company
Victoria Station & Pimlico Railway Company

Appendix III

British Railways Locomotives at 31st December 1948

(i) STEAM (STANDARD GAUGE)

CLASSIFICATION BY POWER—POUNDS OF TRACTIVE EFFORT

Function and Type	Up to 20,000	Over 20,000 up to 25,000	Over 25,000 up to 30,000	Over 30,000 up to 35,000	Over 35,000	TOTAL
	No.	No.	No.	No.	No.	No.
Passenger Tender	960	685	400	315	167	2,527
Passenger Tank	1,211	136	—	—	—	1,347
Mixed Traffic Tender ...	203	290	2,124	565	45	3,317
Mixed Traffic Tank ...	481	1,511	110	60	—	2,162
Freight Tender	1,305	2,130	1,478	1,730	313	6,956
Freight Tank	1,308	1,985	293	233	34	3,853
Miscellaneous	49	—	—	—	—	49
TOTAL	5,517	6,737	4,495	2,903	559	20,211

CLASSIFICATION BY WHEEL ARRANGEMENT

Type	Wheel Arrangement	Number		Empty Weight Tons
Steam Tender Locomotives	2-10-0	25		1,751
	0-10-0	1		68
	2-8-0	1,983		130,851
	0-8-0	890		49,448
	4-6-4	1		98
	4-6-2	342		29,653
	4-6-0	2,575		175,833
	2-6-2	186		15,345
	2-6-0	1,027		61,283
	0-6-0	4,210		177,488
	4-4-2	33		2,118
	4-4-0	1,504		77,548
	2-4-0	23		841
			12,800	
Steam Tank Locomotives	4-8-0	17		1,141
	0-8-4	13		949
	2-8-2	54		3,963
	2-8-0	151		10,087
	0-8-2	5		299
	0-8-0	22		1,218
	4-6-2	131		9,047
	2-6-4	638		45,068
	2-6-2	785		46,493
	0-6-4	5		281
	0-6-2	1,190		58,539
	0-6-0	3,010		111,509
	4-4-2	250		13,558
	2-4-2	233		10,347
	0-4-4	562		24,516
	2-4-0	11		354
	0-4-2	113		3,889
	0-4-0	187		4,174
			7,377	
Garratt Locomotives	2-8-8-2	1		139
	2-6-6-2	33		3,963
Total Steam Locomotives		—	20,211	1,071,859
Tenders for Steam Locomotives		—	12,984	—

(ii) ELECTRIC, DIESEL-ELECTRIC AND PETROL LOCOMOTIVES (STANDARD GAUGE)

Type	Function	No.	Current and Voltage	Wheel Type	Horse Power (One-hour rating)	Tractive Effort (lbs.)	Empty Weight Tons
Electric　　..	Passenger	1	DC 1,500v	4-6-4	1,800	16,000	107
	Mixed Traffic	3	,,　　660v	Co-Co	1,470	45,000	298
	Mixed Traffic	1	,,　1,500v	Bo-Bo	1,740	38,000	88
	Freight	9	,,　1,500v	Bo-Bo	1,100	28,000	670
	Freight	1	,,　1,500v	Bo-Bo	1,256	37,600	75
	Freight	2	,,　　660v	Bo-Bo	640	25,000	112
		17					1,350
Diesel-Electric　..	Passenger	2	DC　720v	Co-Co	1,600	41,400	245
	Freight	1	,,　640v	0-6-0	250	24,000	38
	Freight	3	,,　430v	0-6-0	350	30,000	144
	Freight	47	,,　430v	0-6-0	350	35,000	2,272
	Freight	1	,,　400v	0-6-0	350	30,240	48
	Freight	6	,,　430v	0-6-0	350	33,500	258
	Freight	3	,,　460v	0-6-0	350	30,000	155
	Freight	4	,,　400v	0-6-0	350	32,000	189
		67					3,349
Petrol　..　　..	Freight	2	—	0-4-0	40	7,500	16
TOTAL		86					4,715

(iii) SUMMARY OF LOCOMOTIVE STOCK

Type	Number	Empty Weight Tons
Steam　　..　　..　　..　　..	20,211	1,071,859
Electric　　..　　..　　..　　..	17	1,350
Diesel-Electric　　..　　..　　..	67	3,349
Petrol　　..　　..　　..　　..	2	16
Service　　..　　..　　..　　..	50	1,292
Total Standard Gauge　　..	20,347	1,077,866
Non-Standard Gauge　　..	5	97
Total (all types)　　..	20,352	1,077,963

Appendix IV

British Railways Coaching Traffic Vehicles at 31st December 1948

(i) NUMBER OF VEHICLES

	1st Class	2nd Class	3rd Class	Composite	Restaurant Cars	Sleeping Cars	TOTAL
PASSENGER CARRIAGES, INCLUDING RAIL MOTOR VEHICLES							
Steam*	1,541	18	25,251	8,318	628	365	36,121
Electric	95	—	3,509	582	46	—	4,232
TOTAL	1,636	18	28,760	8,900	674	365	40,353

	Post Office Vans	Luggage, Parcel, Milk, Fruit and Brake Vans	Fish Vans and Trucks	Carriage Trucks	Horse Boxes	Miscellaneous	TOTAL
NON-PASSENGER CARRYING							
Steam*	147	6,231	3,699	2,008	2,482	743	15,310
Electric		3	—	—	—	—	3
TOTAL	147	6,234	3,699	2,008	2,482	743	15,313

(ii) NUMBER OF SEATS OR BERTHS

	Passenger Carriages			Restaurant Cars			Sleeping Cars	
	1st Class	2nd Class	3rd Class	1st Class	2nd Class	3rd Class	1st Class	3rd Class
Steam*	215,912	832	1,850,523	7,041	18	12,079	2,097	5,074
Electric	21,997	—	299,885	510	—	784	—	—
TOTAL	237,909	832	2,150,408	7,551	18	12,863	2,097	5,074

(iii) LIGHTING FACILITIES OF STEAM STOCK†

	Electrically Lighted		Gas Lighted		Oil Lighted		Not Lighted		TOTAL NUMBER
	Number	% of Total	Number	% of Total	Number	% of Total	Number	% of Total	
STEAM VEHICLES*									
Passenger carrying	34,409	95.26	1,695	4.69	1	—	16	0.05	36,121
Non-passenger carrying	4,374	28.57	1,991	13.00	1,691	11.05	7,254	47.38	15,310
TOTAL	38,783	75.41	3,686	7.16	1,692	3.29	7,270	14.14	51,431

* Includes vehicles used for all types of traction other than electric.
† All electric vehicles are electrically lighted.

Appendix V

British Railways Freight Traffic Vehicles at 31st December 1948

	Merchandise Wagons		Mineral Wagons	Special Wagons	Cattle Trucks	Rail and Timber Trucks	TOTAL
	Open	Covered					
Under 10 tons							
Fitted	4	5,032	—	21	1,964	—	7,021
Non-fitted	7,465	1,118	9,273	6	745	1,088	19,695
TOTAL	7,469	6,150	9,273	27	2,709	1,088	26,716
10 tons and under 14 tons							
Fitted	41,567	72,230	35	48	6,802	220	120,902
Non-fitted	269,807	63,730	527,039	501	1,578	19,231	881,886
TOTAL	311,374	135,960	527,074	549	8,380	19,451	1,002,788
14 tons and under 17 tons							
Fitted	149	1	—	11	—	—	161
Non-fitted	1,196	48	62,418	324	—	1,432	65,418
TOTAL	1,345	49	62,418	335	—	1,432	65,579
17 tons and under 20 tons							
Fitted	5	—	—	—	—	—	5
Non-fitted	2	48	3,060	20	—	—	3,130
TOTAL	7	48	3,060	20	—	—	3,135
20 tons and under 25 tons							
Fitted	19	99	23	87	—	464	692
Non-fitted	390	290	45,157	338	—	13,069	59,244
TOTAL	409	389	45,180	425	—	13,533	59,936
25 tons and over							
Fitted	51	86	30	110	—	23	330
Non-fitted	82	—	515	650	—	5,465	6,712
TOTAL	133	86	545	760	—	5,488	7,012
All Capacities							
Fitted	41,795	77,448	88	277	8,766	707	129,081
Non-fitted	278,942	65,234	647,462	1,839	2,323	40,285	1,036,085
TOTAL	320,737	142,682	647,550	2,116	11,089	40,992	1,165,166
Total Tonnage Capacity	3,923,501	1,636,032	8,100,512	48,837	115,078	736,442	14,560,402
Average Tonnage Capacity per per Vehicle	12.23	11.47	12.51	23.08	10.38	17.97	12.50
BRAKE VANS							
Fitted							2,884
Non-fitted							11,354
TOTAL							14,238

Fitted vehicles are equipped with the automatic continuous brake or through pipe which permits such vehicles to form trains fully controlled by the automatic continuous brake.

Non-fitted vehicles are equipped with hand brakes only.

Appendix VI

British Railways Service Vehicles at 31st December 1948

	Fitted	Non-fitted	Total	Total Tonnage Capacity	Average Tonnage Capacity per Vehicle
WITH TONNAGE CAPACITY					
Locomotive Coal Wagons					
Under 14 tons	—	8,704	8,704	—	—
14 tons and under 17 tons	—	835	835	—	—
17 tons and under 20 tons . .	—	—	—	—	—
20 tons and over	25	8,593	8,618	—	—
Total Locomotive Coal Wagons	25	18,132	18,157	294,899	16.24
Ash and Sand Wagons . .	—	168	168	1,507	8.97
Ballast Wagons	837	8,574	9,411	133,812	14.22
Timber Rail and Sleeper . .	87	1,444	1,531	30,467	19.90
Miscellaneous*	831	3,274	4,105*	14,233	10.21
WITHOUT TONNAGE CAPACITY					
Ballast Brake Vans . .	225	349	574		
Breakdown Cranes . .	124	40	164		
Mess and Tool Vans . .	1,179	852	2,031		
Gasholder Trucks . .	435	24	459		
Travelling Cranes . .	188	498	686		
TOTAL SERVICE VEHICLES	3,931	33,355	37,286		

* Only 1,394 miscellaneous service vehicles have tonnage capacity.

Fitted vehicles are equipped with the automatic continuous brake or through pipe which permits such vehicles to form trains fully controlled by the automatic continuous brake.

Non-fitted vehicles are equipped with hand brakes only.

Appendix VII

Summary of BR Traction and Rolling Stock at 31st December 1988

LOCOMOTIVES

Diesel Shunters	. .	478
Diesel Trains (incl. 197 HST) . .		1,664
Electric ac	. . . .	183
Electric dc	. . . .	47
Steam	. . . .	4

TOTAL	2,376

COACHES

Locomotive-Hauled Passenger		2,677
Locomotive-Hauled Non-Passenger		1,293
High Speed Train Coaches	. .	712

TOTAL	4,862

MULTIPLE UNITS

DMU Passenger	. . . .	2,276
DMU Non-Passenger	. .	32
EMU Passenger	. . . .	7,117
EMU Non-Passenger	. .	25

TOTAL	9,450

REVENUE EARNING FREIGHT

TOTAL	26,279

SERVICE VEHICLES (LIVESTOCK ANALYSIS)

TOTAL	22,074
TOTAL FLEET SIZE	64,861

Comparison with BR at time of Nationalisation

		1948	1988
No. of locomotives . .	. .	20,352	2,376
No. of carriages	. . . .	55,666	14,312
No. of wagons	. . . .	1,216,690	48,353

PRIVATE OWNER FIGURES IN 1988

Locomotives (incl. main line steam)	40
Coaches	137
UK wagons	13,401
Ferry boat wagons	312

Bibliography

Ahrons, E.L., 'Histories of Famous Locomotive Builders', series of articles in *The Engineer*, Vols 129-136.

Allen, C.J., *The London and North Eastern Railway* (Ian Allan).

Bagnell, P.S., *The History of the National Union of Railwaymen* (George Allen & Unwin, 1963).

Berdrow, W., *The Krupps, 1797-1937* (Verlag fur Sozialpolitik, Wirtschaft und Statistik, 1937).

Bonavia, M.R., *The Economics of Transport* (Nisbet/Cambridge University Press, 1936).

Bonavia, M.R., *The Organisation of British Railways* (Ian Allan, 1971).

Bonavia, M.R., *The Birth of British Rail* (George Allan & Unwin, 1979).

Bonavia, M.R., *The Four Great Railways* (David & Charles, 1980).

Bonavia, M.R., *British Rail: The First 25 Years* (David & Charles, 1981).

Bonavia, M.R., *The History of the LNER*, Vols 1 and 2 (George Allen & Unwin, 1982); Vol 3 (George Allen & Unwin, 1983).

Bond, R.C., *A Lifetime with Locomotives* (Goose & Son, 1975).

Brown, F.A.S., *Sir Nigel Gresley, Locomotive Engineer* (Ian Allan, 1962).

Bulleid, H.A.V., *Master Builder of Steam* (Ian Allan, 1983).

Cox, E.S., *Locomotive Panorama*, Vols 1 and 2 (Ian Allan, 1965).

Cox, E.S., *British Railways Standard Steam Locomotives* (Ian Allan), 1966).

Darwin, B., *A Century of Medical Service: The Swindon Medical Fund Society* (Swindon Press, 1947).

Doughar, D., *Sir William Armstrong – The Great Gunmaker* (Frank Graham, Newcastle-upon-Tyne, 1970).

Gale, W.K.V., *Iron and Steel* (The Moorland Publishing Co., Ashbourne, 1977).

Hume, K.J., *History of Engineering Metrology* (Mechanical Engineering Publications, 1980).

Johnson, J., and R.A. Long, *British Railways Engineering, 1948-80* (Mechanical Engineering Publications, 1981).

Kelley, T., *George Birkbeck: The Creator of the Mechanics Institutes* (Liverpool University Press, 1957).

Larkin, E.J., *Works Organization and Management* (Pitman, 1st edn 1940; 2nd edn 1945).

Larkin, E.J., *The Elements of Workshop Training* (Pitman, 1st edn 1945; reprinted 1946; 2nd edn 1947).

Larkin, E.J., *Memoirs of a Railway Engineer* (Mechanical Engineering Publications, 1979).

Larkin, E.J., and J.G., *The Railways Workshops of Britain 1823–1986* (Macmillan Press, 1988).

Low, R.C.S. 'The Re-organisation of British Railways Workshops', *Journal of Institution of Locomotive Engineers*, 1967.

Lowe, J.W., *British Steam Locomotive Builders* (Goose & Son, 1975).

Marsden, C.J. *B.R.E.L Life & Times Series* (Oxford Publishing Company, 1990).

Mountford, E., *Caerphilly Works, 1901–1964* (Roundhouse Books, 1965).

Nock, O.S., *Sir William Stanier, An Engineering Biography* (Ian Allan, 1966).

Nock, O.S., *History of the Great Western Railway* (Ian Allan, 1964).

Nock, O.S., *Two miles a Minute* (Patrick Stephens, 1980).

Nock, O.S., (gen. ed.) *Encyclopaedia of Railways* (Octopus, 1977).

Peck, A.S., *The Great Western at Swindon Works* (Oxford Publishing Company, 1983).

Radford, J.B., *Derby Works and Midland Locomotives* (Ian Allan, 1971).

Reed, B., *Crewe Locomotive Works and its Men* (David & Charles, 1982).

Rogers, H.C.B. *The Last Steam Locomotive Engineer: R.A. Riddles* (George Allan & Unwin, 1970).

Rogers, H.C.B., *Riddles and the '9Fs'* (Ian Allan, 1982).

Round the Works of Our Great Railways (Arnold, 1893).

Skeat, W.O., *George Stephenson and His Letters* (Mechanical Engineering Publications, 1973).

Smith, S.A.S., 'The British Railways Mechanised Iron Foundry, Horwich', *Journal of Institution of Locomotive Engineers*, 1955.

Talbot, E., *A Pictorial Tribute to Crewe Works in the Age of Steam*, (Oxford Publishing Company, 1987).

Thomas, J., *The Springburn Story: The History of the Scottish Railway Metropolis* (David & Charles, 1964).

Vaughan, J., *B.R.E.L. Locomotive Works* (Oxford Publishing Company, 1981).

Warder, S.B., 'Electric Traction in the British Railways Modernisation Plan', *Journal of Institution of Civil Engineers*, Vol. 18, 1961.

Warren, J.G.H., *A Century of Locomotive Building, Robert Stephenson & Company, 1823–1923* (Andrew Reid & Co., 1923).

Wilson, R.B., *Sir Daniel Gooch: Memoirs and Diary* (David & Charles, 1972).

Wilson and Reader, *Men and Machines: History of D. Napier and Son, 1808–1958* (Weidenfeld & Nicolson, 1958).

Young, R., *Timothy Hackworth* (Shildon 'Stockton & Darlington Railway' Jubilee Committee, Shildon Town Council Office, County Durham, 1975).

The 'Melt Shop', Crewe Works c1962, where locomotives were cut up for scrap.   *(Colin J. Marsden Collection)*

—— ooΟoo ——